Heretic Café

When church people use God

To manipulate us.

How to fight back and

Thrive!

Selma Kerren

The Stanton Book Company

Heretic Café
Copyright © 2013 by Selma Kerren

The Stanton Book Company
Fair Oaks, California

ISBN-13: 978-1496122797
ISBN-10: 1496122798

Printed in the United States of America

About the Author

Other works by Selma Kerren:

A Cry in the Wilderness
The Raw Confessions of Texas Seven's Joseph Garcia

And

KDRAMA! The House of X
A story of love, betrayal and a fairytale ending.

Preface

I was tinkering around on the internet one freezing, January morning back in 2006, with my television turned to Trinity Broadcast Network. From my desk in Orange County, California, I could see that America was still reeling in the aftermath of Hurricane Katrina…and that's when I heard it.

"God was laughing when they died!"

I looked up and saw two, coiffed preachers talking about the countless victims who died during Hurricane Katrina. Then they started in on the victims of 9/11 and the 2004 Tsunami, as though dishing around Super Bowl scores. That was the defining moment. I had enough.

This book comes about as a result of several inflammatory statements made by American televangelists who claimed on worldwide television that the victims of recent disasters basically 'had it coming.' A few moments later, concerning Katrina's dead, the second preacher said:

"They were all pimps and prostitutes, anyway!"

Rhetoric such as this is nothing new coming from Christian and Catholic clergy. For centuries they peddled this kind of tripe against mankind, whether we deserved it or not. They dare to allege that God enjoys watching the loss of life and limb, of the guilty and innocent alike, no matter how inexplicable or unfair. "God is God," they'll tell you. "He does it because He loves us!" Listen to them long enough and you'll start to believe them.

As an avid churchgoer of thirty-five years, I happen to know for a fact that the televangelists' statements that morning were a total fraud. Christ and the Apostles never said any such thing against people in distress, or 'sinners' for that matter. And what really chaps my hide is that no one ever bothers to check and see if such statements are actually in the Testaments, not even the media. Everyone just keeps on drinkin' the Kool-Aid.

Hysterically, the televangelists in question have yet to acknowledge that the majority of Katrina victims were the elderly, the disabled and hospitalized persons, most of them black and poor, while another 94,000 victims of the Tsunami were toddlers and school-aged children. And God was laughing when they died? You're about to discover that nothing of the sort is true. Welcome to the **Heretic Café.**

The things we'll be exposing in this book might have caused us to be burned at the stake five hundred years ago. Lucky for us, we can discuss anything we like today, absent of inquisition and torture; hence the provocative title. Over the centuries, many fraudulent doctrines concerning the Judeo-Christian God became canonized (cemented in stone), and when forced upon the famished commoner, resulted in irreversible, mental health disorders and, more egregious, a sickly fear of God; for billions more a permanent separation from Christ. This book will highlight the most dangerous, soul-crushing ones.

For instance, ever notice how far too many clinically insane persons display severe a fixation on Christ and / or the devil? It's a specific mental illness that has its origins in the torture chambers of the medieval church. People in times past who dared question the false doctrines of the church were convicted of heresy and killed. This book presents evidence in **support** of these 'heretics.'

As we take on one false doctrine after another, you will be surprised to learn that the church's mainstream teachings on judgment, disasters, punishment and human suffering are actually **not supported** by the New Testament at all.

While it is true that Christ and the Apostles warned numerous times that Judgment Day will come, you will learn that judgment has not yet begun. In fact, it is being deliberately **delayed, deferred and set aside** until that designated moment.

So, who or what really 'sent' those recent disasters? Was it God? ... man's own negligence? ... or some other violent, unseen entity that likes to dress up like God? Whatever it was, it seems to enjoy killing the weak while sparing the strong.

You will also be surprised to learn that many Bible scriptures concerning human suffering were purposely **altered** after the original Apostles died; no doubt to strike fear in us all and control the whole world. And, because no one was allowed to question those obfuscations, many of

Christ's original teachings are perhaps buried forever.

Instead, opposite-doctrines emerged with strangleholds on the church, some of which made their way into the secular conscience also. For instance, one can hardly sign a contract without clauses alleging the 'Acts of God.'

The obfuscations in question are, in fact, so entrenched in the modern-day human psyche, if one tries to bring them to the attention of church leadership, the backlash is practically hostile. Consequently, this book exposes how incredibly fraudulent the false doctrines are, by using the preachers' own game. Bible scripture.

Here's how it works: this book speaks strictly about the Judeo-Christian God, and none other. If you want to know what Buddha said about something, you'll have to read the book of Buddha. If you want to know what Mohammed said, you'll have to read his book. The same applies to the Hindi, Sikh, Hare Krishna, Scientology, Mormon, Kabala, and Satanic bodies of work which, contrary to popular opinion, are not about the same God and do not teach the same things.

Be also advised that this book might prove to be somewhat unsettling for many religious traditionalists, which is exactly the effect intended. They've enjoyed a sordid history of preferring tradition over hardcore facts long enough; therefore, I make no apology. All points raised in this book were cross-checked for accuracy against the original Greek and Hebrew lexicons of Strong's Exhaustive Concordance, Thayer's Greek-English Lexicon, and Sovereign

Grace Publishing's Hebrew-Greek-English Interlinear Bible, all of which cry the same data.

In other words, the contentions presented in this book are forensic in nature and cannot be argued with.

Heretic Cafe was written in an evangelical style for the express purpose of communicating with non-Christians on the most basic level. Many of the scriptures have been purposely presented in a short, easy-to-read tempo to keep from clouding the issues; and yet, not one iota of the original meaning was altered.

For many, this book won't mean a hill of beans right now but will speak volumes on the day your doctor announces you've got three months to live, or your child turns up missing, your house burns to the ground. On that day, you'll look up to the sky and question, "Why? What have I done?"

Predictably, your spiritual advisors will try to sell you the old God-is-trying-to-teach-you-something gimmick. And what about this oldie-but-goodie? "All things happen for a reason."

That's when you'll remember some of this cheeky back-talk as though your life depends on it. So, grab a cup of coffee and join me inside the Heretic Café.

Dedication

Special thanks to my beloved mother and her husband, of Surfers' Paradise, Australia, for their enduring and always fun presence in my life.

Many thanks also to the Reverend Charles Capps, of England, Arkansas, whose own books started me thinking...

Table of Contents

Since the start of the New Testament Age, God is no longer in the punishment business.

If He were, we'd all be dead.

Myth 1

Disasters.

Are They Really

Judgments From God?

God...disasters...and you. These are the axioms of our time. September 11, the Tsunami and Hurricane Katrina: were they God's judgments? Does God really send disasters to punish us? Many televangelists say so.

The world has been subjected to this type of indoctrination for hundreds of years, and has gone uncontested just as long. Recent events, however, raised new levels of debate from Main Street to Wall Street, the boardroom to the bedroom, your house to the White House; not to mention countless documentaries.

For the purpose of this chapter, we will use Hurricane Katrina as our model disaster, and compare the true words of Christ against the claims of several American televangelists.

In the days ensuing Hurricane Katrina, President George W. Bush addressed the nation and announced that America was being tested. This was a true statement, but according to the New Testament, the Judeo-Christian God was **not** the one sending the tests. Simultaneously, American televangelists and Christian commentators alleged on world-wide television that the victims of recent disasters were "killed by God as punishment for their sins."

Such abhorrent claims deserve vigorous public contest, as does the willful obfuscation of Christ's true words, which are regularly bastardized at the pulpit for the express purpose of frightening the world. As a result, the fracture between God and man is compounded every Sunday morning as we wade, hip-deep, through the quagmire of Bible scripture, in an effort to disconnect the old-church muck from the truth.

The Big Policy Change

For instance, it is common knowledge among the clergy that since the crucifixion of Christ, a definite shift occurred concerning judgment. In fact, it was an entire change of policy. The Old Testament narratives present a foreboding and punishing God wherein animal sacrifice, polygamy, and bone-crunching retribution are frequent episodes. After the crucifixion, however, these practices were quickly abolished and replaced with a lighter, easier outreach, such as: forgiveness, spiritual autonomy (the right of every person to access God without priest-intrusion), the immediate end of animal sacrifice and human punishment; and yet the clergy persists.

Many preachers will now attempt to cite several deaths that are listed in the New Testament after the crucifixion, as 'proof' they were killer strikes from God. Upon closer inspection, however, those deaths were either self-induced, or came about as a result of murder at the hands of humans. And this is where so many preachers fail to make the connection. They fail to properly identify where disasters come from.

As a result, mankind has come to believe the Judeo-Christian God hates us, and wants to harm us for no good reason, while the church's public image is that of the crazed mother in Stephen King's film, *Carrie*.

We've all encountered people like that; they're all over. The problem is Christ never gave them permission to act that way, as we will soon find out. Hysterically, no one, including the media, ever bothers to check if the church's claims are true.

Pass the Kool-Aid.

Ringing The Dinner Bell

Take for instance the New Orleans levy breach. No doubt this occurred because the levies were **built incorrectly** forty years earlier. After repeated warnings from lone structural engineers, critics in the federal government continued to turn a blind eye since the early 1960s, and neglected to make the necessary repairs. Knowing perfectly well the levies could never withstand a killer hurricane, the government practically rang the dinner bell for disaster.

The tiny nation of Holland, on the other hand, lies beneath sea level and is engulfed by water on three sides. In 1953, a major storm breached a large network of their levies, killing 2,000 people. Unlike the U.S., Holland quickly made the necessary repairs, and although many more bad weather systems hit, suffered no more damages.

Also interesting to note is that Holland legalized prostitution and marijuana use in 2000. Although Dutch lawmakers acknowledged in 2008 that passing these initiatives caused noticeable spikes in crime, no recent 'killer strikes from God' are on record.

In any case, Holland's levies were **repaired correctly.** Therefore, to say the flooding of New Orleans was an 'Act of God' is ludicrous. It would be truer to say the New Orleans levy breach was the negligent 'Act of Man'.

The televangelists in question also alleged that the terror attacks of September 11 were the 'Acts of God'. Preachers who say such things are woefully misguided. Repeatedly, they fail to acknowledge one key ingredient, more powerful than the atom bomb.

The missing ingredient is the most deadly weapon of mass destruction in the entire universe! It has the ability to maim, kill and devastate permanently and irreversibly. Once it strikes, there is no turning back. That ingredient is:

Free Will. Ever heard of it?

Free will, when used for evil, creates permanent devastation that cannot be reversed. The Holocaust of World War II is one example. The Sudan slave crisis is another, as are rape, murder and mayhem in general. The bottom line is: before we pin a murder rap on God, let's first check to see if man had anything to do with it.

Now, one can understand how the 2004 Tsunami could be misconstrued as an 'Act of God' since man had nothing to do with this. However, 95,000 children died in that flood, all of whom did nothing to deserve it, and yet many preachers persist in making this claim. They know perfectly well that if God wants to snuff someone out, in this New Testament era, He would never kill innocent children in the process. He's a better shot than that. Obviously, the televangelists' claims are hopelessly flawed and other explanations must be sought.

Wardrobe Malfunction

The televangelists in question, that January morning were Perry Stone and Joe Van Koevering. Now, let's review the full catalog of their inflammatory remarks against the disaster victims.

"God rode inside that wind with a prophetic message for those people!"

"They're all just murderers and prostitutes, anyway!"

"If you don't obey God's commandments, the Bible says He will appoint terror unto you!"

"Anyone who says any different is a false prophet, and the antichrist is speaking through him!"

Other commentators, like acclaimed author and former U.S. treasury agent, John McTernan, said on the Daystar network:

"God sent Katrina and other disasters because the White House coerced Israel into giving up more of its land."

And finally, like countless pastors around America, John Hagee of San Antonio, Texas, said:

"They got exactly what they deserve!"

That month, TBN's legal office was contacted for comment to see if the network actually endorsed those remarks. Only their department secretary made herself available. She said, "TBN can't control everything our hosts say on air from moment to moment."

Yes, but they might try editing their programs before airing them, if only for liability's sake. For instance, official statistics and televised footage defy the preachers' claims. Known pimps and prostitutes *were not* among the dead.

In August of 2007, TBN executives were invited a second time to clarify their position, and again no response was received.

We are now left to assume they actually endorse those remarks, which only serves to confuse their staple message. Since TBN's inception in the early 1970s, its town-cry has always been, "God loves us **despite our sins.**"

Nevertheless, the network allowed its hosts to announce publicly that the Judeo-Christian God "killed" the victims of all three disasters, as did two other major Christian networks: Day Star and Sky Angel. TBN executives also refused to explain this incredible remark, which prompted this book:

"And God was laughing when they died!"

In 2003, TBN co-founder Jan Crouch found herself battling colon cancer. Everyone agrees that contracting a deadly disease is the undisputed 'personal disaster' of anyone's lifetime, so Jan's ordeal was no laughing matter.

The problem is, the entire Christian community knows that since the crucifixion, the Judeo-Christian God harbors no favorites **of any kind.** Therefore, if He laughs at one person (allegedly), He laughs at us all when disaster strikes.

Hence, following through on the preachers' claims, God was also laughing at Jan Crouch when her personal disaster hit. Why is it the network couldn't see the quagmire it created by allowing that remark on air? Perhaps the incident had become a wardrobe malfunction that TBN executives could not reconcile.

Match Point

OK preachers, we see your ten, and raise you fifty. The next ten exhibits stipulate what Christ *really* said about judgment and disasters:

1) John 5:22

"The Father judges no one, but has committed all judgment to Me."

2) John 12:47

"If anyone hears My words and rejects them, I will not judge them, for I didn't come to judge, but to save the world."

Notice that Christ stated He was given the right to allocate judgment as He saw fit, but politely declined, even when people rejected Him to the face; symbolic perhaps of the party-loving people of New Orleans.

It is also a well-known fact among Christians that when the Judeo-Christian God spoke a thing, it was meant for all time, applicable to every age and civilization. This means in Christ there is no space or time, only continuum.

Albert Einstein looked into the universe and identified this continuum as one of the aspects of *The Theory of Relativity*. The Apostle Paul explained it this way:

3) Hebrews 13:8

"Jesus Christ is the same yesterday, today and forever."

Following through on this principle of infinity, God's standard of declining to judge, punish and kill after the crucifixion, applies also to the people of today. To fortify this point let's look at another example:

One day, Jesus and the disciples were walking the long, hot road toward Jerusalem, when they passed a village of Samaritans. They tried to enter for food and water, but the villagers wouldn't let them in, due to 'ethnic differences'. Very angered by this effrontery, the disciples tried to coerce Jesus into exacting punishment against them, but notice His shocking reaction:

> 4) Luke 9:52-56
> "Master, do you want us to command destruction to come down on them?" But He **rebuked them**, and said, "You don't know what kind of [**demon**] **spirit** you are speaking from! I didn't come to destroy men, but to save them!"

How much plainer can it get? The New Testament Christ did not appreciate this kind of talk back then, and since He never changes, He certainly wouldn't now. In fact, He called this type of behavior 'demonized'. In short, Christ read them the riot act for talking like that, and yet the church persists along this line.

Evil's Big Reveal

If we are to take into consideration the words of Christ and the Apostles, we should acknowledge all they said, not just some of it; otherwise we might be accused of selective affectation. Christ identified Satan as the true killer of humankind, and the actual causer of natural disasters. (You know Satan, don't you?...'Carries a pitchfork...wears a little red suit.)

Although the topic of devils and demons is politically unsexy, perhaps we should consider paying attention if Christ tried to warn us about an unseen killer on the loose.

Mainstream church leaders decline to give us this information because they are afraid of ridicule. Since Flip Wilson's 1970 jingle, *The Devil Made Me Do It,* the unseen predator has been allowed to run amuck and go deeper into hiding, while the Judeo-Christian God takes a rap for every disaster this marauder per-petrates, on the global and personal level. Take a look:

5) John 10:10

The thief comes only to **steal, kill, and destroy**, but I have come to give them Life more abundantly.

In this one, small statement, Christ finally clears it all up. The 'thief' is Satan, identified here as the true killer of all mankind.

What you believe on this matter is your own business. The point is: what mainstream preachers say on worldwide television about judgment and disasters, simply does not match scripture.

Smart critics will now argue that it's absurd to blame the devil for all of humanity's crimes and chaos. That's a valid point and should be addressed. They may rest assured that God is not ignorant in the matter of our accountability, hence the soon coming Judgment Day. In the meantime, Christ and the Apostles repeatedly identified Satan as the true cause of all evil, including: poverty, disease, chaos, rape, murder, injustice, freak accidents, tragedies, and natural disasters of every kind.

More alarming, they said that Satan knows when to strike, and make it look as though the Judeo-Christian God did it. Take a look:

6) 2nd Corinthians 11:14

And is it any wonder, because Satan disguises himself as an angel of light...

Trauma can alter our paths in life forever, break us down beyond repair, and cause generational hardships, the insidious effects of which, many times begin in early childhood. For this reason it's very important to know who does what, and where disasters come from.

The Deferred Payment Plan

Regretfully, this book cannot purport that Judgment Day will never come. On the contrary, Christ and the Apostles clearly said it is coming, and will be more terrifying than anything we can possibly imagine. However, the point of this chapter is to prove that actual judgment has not yet begun. Take a look:

7) John 12:48(b)

...the words that I have spoken will judge them **on the last day.**

8) 2nd Peter 3:7

But the heavens and earth...are being **preserved** and **reserved** for the day...of judgment...

Notice that the Apostle Peter said judgment is being delayed, deferred and set aside. Many people harbor an unhealthy fear of judgment, but that day does not have to be a bad thing.

Don't forget, judgment can also be a good thing. It can bring large cash settlements in court. Further, the parents of missing children are going to find out what happened to them, so on and so forth.

And now, from Matthew Chapter 13, comes **ironclad evidence** from Christ's own mouth that disasters are not sent by the Judeo-Christian God, not yet, anyway.

9) Matthew 13:27-41

God saw that many of the people had become evil, so He said to His angels, **"An enemy has corrupted them."** So the angels said to him, "Do you want us to destroy those evil ones?" But God said, **"No, don't destroy them just yet,** in case you upset the good people in the process. Let both grow together **until Judgment Day..."**

There is very little that critics can do or say to dispute the meaning of this statement. (The above passage is presented with the interpretation inserted.) Here, Christ declared that no world-wide judgment will occur **until Judgment Day** and shuts down all further arguments on the matter.

Notice also that Christ does, in fact, blame 'the enemy' (which is 'Satan' in Bible-speak) for mankind's corruption.

From this we can be sure, once and for all, that the Judeo-Christian God never sent disasters of any kind upon anyone since the crucifixion, for the simple reason that Judgment has not yet begun.

Technically, it could now be said that anyone who claims otherwise, defies God's own statements.

Hell or High Water

The televangelists' inflammatory remarks against disaster victims have now been quickly reduced to nothing more than ignorant slander. When juxtaposed against the true words of Christ, their remarks serve no other purpose than to further victimize certain groups of people, who were predisposed to hardships from the time they were born.

To amplify this point, let's take a closer look at the profiles of those who actually perished during Hurricane Katrina, according to published statistics:

- Elderly men over the age of 75.

- Elderly persons drowning in nursing-home beds.

- Infants dying of dehydration.

- Hospital patients without electricity and life support.

- Disabled persons unable to push their wheelchairs to safety.

- Persons too poor or uninformed to evacuate the area.

Hysterically, all the commentators conveniently failed to mention that the French Quarter…where 'true sinners' congregate to drink, pimp, gamble and fornicate…came away **totally unscathed by flood water;** as proved by news footage.

We contacted a few of the televangelists and asked them why they supposed the French Quarter stayed perfectly dry throughout the hurricane. As the few replies came in, it was difficult to keep a straight face while reading them. One alleged:

> "Well, that's because the French Quarter is situated on higher ground than the rest of the city!"

The commentator said this as though it were possible for 'higher ground' to escape a killer-strike from God. Another didn't answer the question at all and tried to turn the table on us:

> "What exactly are you trying to suggest, here?"

They didn't seem to understand that we were not suggesting anything. Rather, we were confronting them by the actual words of Christ, which seemed to oppose them at every turn of the page. To date, none of the commentators have offered an explanation as to why the Katrina floodwaters spared 'sinners' but killed the innocent.

We hardly need Bible scripture to drive the point all the way home. Had God wanted to judge the people of New Orleans, He would have started with the French Quarter, (also known as the red light district for a reason), and worked his way south to the family parishes, but it never happened that way.

We reminded the televangelists that God is a better shot than that, and never misses His mark. There was no reply to this.

We also pointed out that if God were in the business of handing out just desserts, the Earth would have split open and swallowed up all the slave owners of the Deep South, for their involvement in two hundred years of human trafficking, rape, torture and murder. But this never happened either. Predictably their reply was:

"Well, the Civil War was the Act of God."

No, actually it was not. The Civil War was an Act of Man **finally siding up with God**. There is a big difference between a police action, and a supernatural intervention. When criminals are brought to justice, it is hardly ever an 'Act of God.' Just watch the news. This is because we were given authority to govern ourselves. And now, this final message from Heaven:

10) James 1:16-17

Do not be **deceived**, beloved. Every good and perfect gift is from above…from the Father of Lights, and in Him is **no variation**, nor slightest degree of change.

Oddly, none of the televangelists disputed the 'The Ten Exhibits' referenced in this chapter. And how could they possibly? Their replies were identical and emotional:

"You're reading it wrong!"

"That's not what it means!"

"You're treading on dangerous ground here!"

After careful examination of 'The Ten Exhibits' highlighted in this chapter, we have no choice but to conclude that true judgment has not yet begun. Now might be a good time to consider the possibility that another, unseen force is at work here, one that is super-destructive and well-hidden.

When Christ was born, the Judeo-Christian God said, "Peace on Earth, good will toward men." His New Testament policy will not change toward the people of Earth until the end of days.

Do disasters really come from the Judeo-Christian God?

You be the judge.

Myth 2

Human Suffering.

Is It Really Glorious?

For some reason, church leaders make the repeated claim that human suffering brings 'glory' to one's self and to God. From this comes yet another fraudulent doctrine that you might recognize:

> "He does it because He loves us."

This is probably one of the most heinous church teachings ever perpetrated upon mankind. Invariably, this teaching involves pain, suffering, confusion and anguish. Furthermore, it presents the Judeo-Christian God as a cruel sadist. 'Suffering' in church-speak can mean anything from sickness, disease, poverty, grief and all other kinds of heartbreak. Let's review this false teaching in action.

In January of 2006, Anne Graham-Lotz, the daughter of America's most beloved evangelist, Billy Graham, wrote the most staggering remarks of all on her website. Take a look:

"How has your year begun?

Did you start 2006 with a job layoff?

Miscarriage?…Divorce?…the death of a loved one?

A fatal disease?…Or bankruptcy?

Or, were you the victim of a violent crime?"

Then she wrote…

"Sometimes God wraps His glory in hard circumstances, **grief and suffering,** and it never occurs to us that within them is a **fresh revelation** of Himself."

Such remarks are a complete bastardization of the Judeo-Christian God's true outreach toward man. Mrs. Graham-Lotz dared to suggest that if you met with any of the disasters mentioned above, there was some kind of special message from God hidden inside each one. She further suggests that the special message would not be revealed *unless* one meets with them.

Her remarks are actually so shameful, there was a two-year delay in publishing this book, pending the decision on whether to disclose her name, as was the case with the other televangelists highlighted in this book.

Anne Graham-Lotz, like so many others in the church, implicates God as the *accomplice* to heinous crimes against humanity, and then has the audacity to sell them as 'glorious.'

She never stopped to consider that crime victims, such as the parents of missing children, might one day come across her remarks and be struck in the heart by them. Whatever the case, her message hardly applies to *real* victims.

Take for instance Florida's nine-year old Jessica Lunsford. Jessica was abducted, raped, and murdered in February of 2005, by sex-offender John Evander Couey. Couey raped the nine-year old repeatedly and kept her locked in his closet as she bled, vaginally, for three days. Couey even allowed her to look out the window where she saw police teams searching for her, in the field next to Couey's mobile home. Fearing the police were getting too close, Couey dug a hole in his backyard, told Jessica to step into a trash bag, and buried her alive.

Now, according to Anne Graham-Lotz's summation, there was "glory and fresh revelation wrapped inside" the child's murder, and her parent's utter grief. Anne Graham-Lotz's remarks are a perfect example of church leadership's recklessness when addressing human suffering.

This false teaching had its origin in the Old Testament Book of Job. For those not familiar with him, Job (pronounced 'Jobe' as in 'robe') was the wealthy and somewhat nervous man who lived during Old Testament times in the region of Mesopotamia. In this account, Job's ten children were murdered and livestock stolen, after which he was struck head to toe with painful boils, and all in one day. Concerning these events, he made the following over-the-top, ignorant statements:

Job 1:21(b)
"…The Lord gives, and the Lord takes away…"

Job 13:15
"Though he slay me, yet will I praise Him…"

Now, just because Job's pious soliloquies sound 'holy' does not make them true. The man was delirious with pain and he didn't know what he was saying. He mistakenly believed the Hebrew God had launched the destruction against him.

Furthermore, throughout Chapters 9 and 16, Job accused God of breaking all his bones, tearing him apart with His teeth, and pouring out his kidneys onto the ground. This alone should have raised red flags with theologians, but has never been questioned.

The truth is, Job's understanding of God was completely unhinged. At the end of his ordeal, the man looked back at all he said, and ADMITTED he didn't know the first thing about God. Take a look:

Job 42:3
"…Therefore I said things…which I didn't know anything about."

Job 42.6

"Therefore I hate myself and repent in dust and ashes."

In summary, Job admitted he didn't know God at all, had only 'heard stuff' about Him, and hated himself for all the outrageous gibberish he said about God. And yet the church continues to cite Job as the poster-boy of faith as though suffering were a necessary component of our growth.

Church leadership is well aware that both Testaments are littered with embarrassing crimes and Job's errors are hardly any different. The embarrassing events were included into the permanent record, not so that we should imitate them, but to mark them as 'what not to do'. Take a look:

- After the destruction of Sodom and Gomorra, Lot's daughters got him drunk, had sex with him, and became pregnant by Lot, their own father. Genesis 19:31-36

- Abraham lied about his wife, Sarah, (twice) and said she was his sister, causing her to be confined and manhandled by other men. Genesis 12:15-16 and 20:2

- King David of Israel had a good man killed, so that he could sleep with his wife. 2nd Samuel 11:15

- Israel had allowed idol worship into their society and actually resorted to sacrificing and burning their own children. 2nd Kings 17:17

In conclusion, we can see that just because a Bible figure made a large mistake, does not mean they are to be imitated by us. The above also proves that Job's misnderstanding of the Judeo-Christian God was not only unhinged, but totally disqualified by 'The Exhibits' outlined in the prior chapter. Such allegations should be vigorously contested, preferably in a court of law, if they exasperate the minds of already troubled persons.

Still not convinced? Let's travel further east where suffering increases by the latitude. Militant extremists have systematically butchered and enslaved unarmed villagers in the African nation of Sudan for over twenty years. Whenever villagers dare to fight back, their arms are cut off with machetes to the extent they can no longer take care of themselves.

Our bet is that every one of those villagers will tell Mrs. Graham-Lotz there was no 'fresh revelation' or 'glory' found in any of their wounds.

Myth 3

Bad White House Policies.

Do They Really

Cause Disasters?

This claim sounds good on TV, especially when paired with churchy organ music and a bouffant hairdo, but still fails to match the actual words of Christ and the Apostles. However, unlike many questionable church doctrines, this one actually *does* come with an interesting paper trail.

Discussions about disasters are receiving ample media coverage lately. Documentaries exploring extinction-level events litter the networks practically every week. And with December 21, 2012, as the 'new black' of doomsday predictions, one doesn't know what to think anymore.

Whatever the case, these programs sound the alarm of frightening biological, geological and apocalyptic things to come. By watching them, we can see how deeply rooted the concept of doomsday has crept into the collective human psyche.

In September of 2007, Nebraska State Senator, Ernest Chambers, filed a lawsuit 'against God' in which he accused Him of causing "widespread death, destruction and terrorization of millions…fearsome floods, horrendous hurricanes and terrifying tornadoes." The Senator filed the suit tongue-in-cheek, only to prove a point about frivolous lawsuits. His view of God, however, fits perfectly into mainstream impressions.

Truth v. Shenanigans

Two years earlier in September of 2005, MSNBC anchor, Chris Jansing, hosted *The Ethical Edge: Hurricane Katrina*. Guests on the panel were two professors, a Catholic priest, and a Rabbi from New Orleans. To open the discussion, Ms. Jansing directed a question to the Catholic priest about Katrina casualties.

"But father, why *would* God do something like this to people?"

Predictably, the priest delivered right on cue. "Yes exactly. Why *does* God do these things to people? That's been the age old question!"

The Rabbi, irritated by the remark, set the record straight and promptly reminded the panel that God would never hurt innocent people in this way, and that it was "only a natural disaster." The Rabbi's response was refreshing, since the Jews in general subscribe only to the punishing God of the Old

Testament. After that, it seemed the Catholic priest knew he was not going to get away with any more Dark Ages shenanigans and basically stayed quiet the rest of the program. (All it takes is a little back-talk and the web of lies quickly crumbles.)

We cannot fault Ms. Jansing on this misinformation. She is a young, hard-working journalist, not an ordained minister, and didn't know any better. Like so many around the world, she rightfully looked to church leaders for clear-cut answers. The Catholic priest on the other hand was totally without excuse.

That same week, State Senator Hank Irwin (R-AL), joined in the media fray and told MSNBC anchor, Joe Scarborough, of *Scarborough Country,* that he also believed the hurricane was God's judgment. Joe Scarborough, armed with New Testament scripture of his own, politely reminded the senator of Christ's instructions in Matthew Chapter 25; that charity is the first order of business in times of crises, before finger-pointing. Although Scarborough's insight was acute, it provided no real answers as to who, or what, caused the hurricane.

Senator Irwin then made reference to New Orleans' police corruption and widespread voodoo practices, and how the evil engagements of a handful of people can cause the innocent to die. Agreed. World wars are a prime example.

We sent the 'The Ten Exhibits' outlined in the prior chapter to the senator and asked him to comment. It should be noted that Senator Irwin, a true Southern gentlemen, promptly responded to our emails *personally*; two in total. From his replies, it was clear that he, unlike the televangelists, truly cared for the disaster victims but also did not acknowledge the scriptures.

The Chocolate City Address

In January of 2006, New Orleans Mayor Ray Nagin delivered his now famous *Chocolate City Address,* wherein he stated on national television, "Surely, God is mad at America…He sent us hurricane after hurricane…"

So, just for the purpose of taking a survey, we faxed Mayor Nagin's office a copy of 'The Ten Exhibits' and asked him to reconsider. Then, something remarkable happened. That next day, the Mayor held another press conference, said he was "truly sorry" and withdrew his "statements about God from the day before." Whether this was done in response to our fax is unknown, but he did so with rare savoir-faire.

It seems that people on the street-level understand God's outreach right away, whereas the religious put up an incredible fight.

The One-Two Punch

By now, people all over America are well aware of Christendom's latest allegation, that recent American disasters are directly linked to controversial White House initiatives. This allegation stems from the White House's involvement in encouraging Israel to give up certain portions of its land to the Palestinians.

Christians view this initiative as a monumental blunder, and nothing more than the White House's attempt to use the Holy Land as a bargaining chip, to ease tensions in the Middle East. As a result, Christians believe God struck back at America with disaster after disaster, at every turn of the policy screw. It's a belief based on the account found in Genesis 12:3, wherein God said to Abraham, "And I will bless those who bless you, and curse those who curse you..."

Now, you will be surprised to learn that American disasters have, in fact, **struck in swift, one-two-punch succession,** after every passing of a controversial policy.

Acclaimed author and former U.S treasury agent, John McTernan, wrote several books about this phenomena; the most notable of which is, *God's Final Warning to America*. His findings are fascinating. In fact, the quick, one-two punch is undeniable.

October 21, 1991:   President George H. Bush opens discussions on Israel's land allocations. That same day, 100-foot waves hit New England's coast and damaged the President's own house.

August 23, 1992:   The Israel land discussions resume, and that same day, Hurricane Andrew, said to be the worst natural disaster ever to hit America, brings $30 billion in damage, and leaves 180,000 Floridians homeless.

May 3, 1999:   Yasser Arafat declared Palestine a 'state' with Jerusalem as its 'capital'. Clinton wrote Arafat a letter congratulating him on his 'own land'. That same day, a 316 mph tornado hit Oklahoma and Kansas, said to be the most powerful in U.S. history.

September 27-28, 1998: Secretary of State Madeleine Albright works out the final details for Israel to give initial portions of land to the Palestinians. That same day, Hurricane Georges hit the Gulf Coast at 110 mph, causing $1 billion damage.

August 29, 2005: Bush praised Ariel Sharon in early August for initiating the Gaza withdrawal and evicting all Jewish settlers. One week later, Hurricane Katrina struck the Gulf States.

And the list goes on and on. No wonder Christian commentators are alarmed. Who wouldn't be? So what exactly is going on here? Whenever things come along to cloud the issues, we should refer back to the statements of Christ as outlined in the previous chapter, from which one timeless message emerges. The first is: He doesn't judge, and the second is: He didn't do it.

John 10:10
"The thief [Satan] comes to steal, kill and destroy. But I have come to bring them Life more abundantly."

In fact, we can cut out the above passage, juxtapose it against any crisis we encounter, and bring immediate clarity to any situation. It tells us who does what. One is the taker of life, and the other is the Giver of Life. It's a delineation that clergy across the board repeatedly fail to clarify.

Now, according to Christian doctrine, 'the thief' came out of eternity (before his fall), and is therefore in possession of certain 'intelligence information.' In other words, he knows how things work. He knows when to strike, make it look as though God did it, and bilk it for all it's worth. This verse also merits another look:

2nd Corinthians 11:14
"And is it any wonder, because Satan disguises himself as an angel of light…"

Another way to interpret recent disasters is to question whether America is doing this to itself. For instance, if you push someone out of your front door, is there any reason as to why they should ever come back? In the same respect, if we push the Judeo-Christian out of our society, schools and legislation, should we really expect Him to stick around and protect us? The Judeo-Christian God is also well known for this somewhat irritating policy:

James 4:2(c)
"You have not, because you ask not."

In this New Testament Age of spiritual autonomy, the Judeo-Christian God no longer infringes upon the free will rights of the individual, let alone the majority. In showing God to the front door, are we leaving our borders wide open for attack? Are we grinding our infra and outer-structures down to impotent stumps, until we have no protection left? You be the judge.

Mainstream church leaders fail to grasp that America's own acts of 'sewing and reaping' may ultimately lead to its demise, which has very little to do with God retaliating against this nation. More likely, we'll beat Him to it.

For instance, how is it God's judgment if an individual smokes cigarettes all his life, practices unhealthy eating habits, and dies prematurely of heart disease? The same logic applies on the greater scale concerning this nation. We emailed 'The Ten Exhibits' to this second group of Christian commentators, just for the purpose of this survey, and only one replied:

"If you're trying to say God doesn't punish sinful people, you shouldn't be doing that. It makes people lazy, and think they can do whatever they want."

Interesting to note is that Americans have been doing whatever they want since 1776, so the hell-fire and brimstone message hasn't exactly worked at all. Perhaps it's time to implement another approach? Instead, church leaders would rather sit back and quash God's true outreach and keep on dishing the Kool Aid.

We also pointed out to the commenators how God failed to kill the sinful slave owners of yesteryear's Deep South. The commentators quietly avoided this challenge and never replied.

Israel vs. The Philistines

It is quite evident from countless Bible scriptures, the Judeo-Christian God prefers that Israel should never give up its land to anyone. In fact, God referred to Israel as the Apple of His Eye; in other words, a great source of love and anguish to Him, and that He would bless or curse a nation according to its dealings with Israel.

So, now that the White House has involved itself in Israel's land deals, what exactly are the commentators alleging? Are they saying that America is cursed? Are they reducing America to the same level as Israel's enemy states?

How can this be since **America never once attacked Israel**, nor abandoned the tiny nation since inception? In fact, America has always been Israel's strongest alley since 1948. And yet, the commentators completely ignore this fact, and continue to insist that America's disasters are a result of God's punishment!

Perhaps recent White House initiatives concerning Israel have not been the smartest moves in history, but several points should be taken into consideration before we interpret American disasters as judgments from God.

A. Gestures of Peace:

Perhaps the White House encouraged Israel to give up certain portions of its land as gestures of peace towards the Palestinians, and to give them a homeland of their own?

Question: Since when are gestures of peace 'evil'?

B. Pure Exhaustion:

After fifty years of daily bloodshed, clashes between the Jewish and Muslim cultures became deadlier by the year. Perhaps life and limb eventually became more important to the Israelis, than prophetic discourse, after living as human targets for over fifty years?

> **Question:** If Christians cannot appreciate Israel's daily struggles, perhaps they should send their own children into Israel's wars to 'fulfill prophecy'?

The Big Pink Elephant in the Room

And finally, let's address the big, pink elephant in the room. It's the elephant that Christian commentators refuse to address, even when confronted by the facts. Here's the big, pink elephant:

> **Why has no Arab nation ever been struck with natural disasters?**
>
> **Since the early 1950's, all Arab nations in the Middle East have either attacked, bombed, or funded terrorism against Israel at one time or another, causing untold damage, and loss of Jewish life and limb.**
>
> **And yet, to date, no Arab nation has ever been hit with a natural disaster!**

Is this because true judgment has not yet begun? It's time for Christian commentators to address this incongruity.

Also interesting to note is that America suffered countless, natural disasters **long before** the White House ever got involved in the Israel land deals. Earthquakes, floods, blizzards, hurricanes, tornados, cyclones, black-out dust bowls, meteor hits, and volcanic explosions are recorded by U.S. weather records:

Going all the way back to 1635!

Hence, what have natural disasters to do with the Israeli land deals, if American disaster records go back 376 years?

Whichever way you slice it, America has done nothing to 'curse' Israel. Therefore, the commentators in question have no reason to lump America together with those nations that actually **bombed Israel** for the past fifty years. As of this writing on December 1, 2014, we're still waiting to see a single natural disaster to hit an enemy nation of Israel; and so far, none have come. Is that because true judgment has not yet begun?

In any case, Israel's prophetic discourse has been fulfilled in many other ways, despite its unwise allocation of lands to the Palestinians. The Israelis were restored to their homeland, in an unprecedented, overnight fashion in 1948, and have arguably never lost a war since 1967; also a prophecy fulfilled.

By July of 2007, it was widely reported that the once pristine West Bank lay in ruins in the hands of the Palestinians. Somehow, its new occupants officially reduced the region into a war-torn, pile of absolute rubble.

Myth 4

Purgatory.

Does It Exist?

The answer is: no; definitely not! 'Purgatory' does not exist. The word, idea, and concept of 'Purgatory' are never mentioned in the Old or New Testaments, directly or indirectly.

This teaching is purely a Catholic concoction and was never authorized nor approved by Christ or the Apostles.

When questioned about the suspicious absence of the word 'Purgatory' in the Testaments, the usual Catholic response is, "Well, neither are words like rapture, trinity, cloning, and abortion," thereby implying that the Vatican has license to make up doctrine as it goes along.

However, the contemporary terms in question, can easily be addressed by a preponderance of other Bible scriptures, whereas 'Purgatory' cannot.

The word 'Purgatory' comes from Latin, meaning: to purge, to make clean, and purify. This particular Catholic doctrine stipulates that no one may enter Heaven without an internship in 'Purgatory', where one's soul is allegedly purified by fire and torment. Furthermore, the fires are lit to a greater or lesser degree, as determined by one's goodness or badness in life. The doctrine also teaches that only priests, nuns, and Catholic clergy receive instant entry to heaven, whereas all others do not.

However, the most basic Christian tenet stipulates that Christ's shed blood paid the **entire price** for our sins and, after that, God requires no additional human suffering to enter Heaven. Needless to say, the doctrine of 'Purgatory' presents glaring incongruities against the original Christian teaching.

So, which is true, and which is the fabrication? Who gave the Vatican permission to add its own gruesome requirements to Christ's easy terms for salvation?

The doctrine of 'Purgatory' also demands that the more one suffers in this life, the less time is required in 'Purgatory', which explains the centuries-old, Catholic fixation with suffering. It's also one of the reasons why the Vatican took it upon itself to torture and murder countless, so-called 'heretics' during the Dark Ages. This was done to "help them with their purification."

It is also common knowledge that Catholics harbor sickly fixations for guilt (sins they committed that they just can't let go of). As a result they teach: "All humans must first pay for the original sin in 'Purgatory' before they can enter Heaven."

According to them, the 'original sin' was disobedience committed by mankind; but once again, neither Testament makes any mention of an 'original sin.' Nor do the Testaments mention that humans must continue to pay for sins after death.

Now, Isaiah 14:12-19 does highlight a certain sin that was committed **long before** humans were ever created, which was 'pride'. However, according to Isaiah, 'pride' was committed by Satan while he was yet in Heaven, during his attempt to overthrow God. Hence, the 'original sin' cannot be pinned on humans to pay. Nice try, though.

Most disturbing of all, the Catholic Church teaches that infants are forbidden from entering Heaven unless baptized into the Catholic Church. Another name for this nursery of hell is 'baby limbo'. However, according to the Vatican, there is no guarantee that any baby will ever get into Heaven, baptized or not, because the maniacal doctrine of 'Purgatory' demands that infants must also pay for the 'original sin'!

Hysterically, the Catholic Church refuses to acknowledge one very, in-your-face incident recorded in Luke 23:43. The incident involves Christ nailed to the cross, and the thief hanging next to Him. The thief asked Jesus to have mercy on him, to whom He answered..."Today you will be in Paradise with Me."

Notice that the thief was not baptized into the Catholic Church, nor was he an avid church-goer. The Vatican denies this account and actually dares to teach that the thief went to 'Purgatory' anyway! It's a teaching that has caused Catholics unnecessary psychological and emotional strain for centuries, and in the opinion of this author, is cause for more legal action. Now, let's examine what the Apostle Paul said about our easy entry into Heaven, contrary to the Catholic bastardizations:

Colossians 2:14

"Christ has wiped out the list of requirements against us, took it out of the way, and nailed it to the cross."

The question now begs, if our list of sins has been "wiped out" why does the Catholic Church require additional punishment?

Bad Moon Rising

Interesting to note is that the Apostle Paul found himself fighting off the early trace elements of many rogue doctrines, while he was yet alive!

For instance, every now and then, the early Christian assemblies found themselves inundated by infiltrators, nursing unrequited fixations for pagan religions. Some of them took to beating and cutting themselves (flagellation), as a means of obtaining 'favor' from God.

Paul swiftly exposed this as a depraved practice in many of his epistles, for the simple reason that Christ never asked for it. Christ said suffering was to be His job alone, while Paul said entry to Heaven is a 'free gift' and could not be earned. Take a look:

Ephesians 2:8-9

For by grace you have been saved through faith...it is the gift of God; not as a result of your working for it, just in case someone wants to boast.

Nevertheless, by the second century, the practice of flagellation reemerged stronger than ever, since the original Apostles were no longer alive to condemn the practice.

Simultaneously, early Catholic practitioners were able to canonize 'Purgatory' as an official doctrine, and include it into its modern-day Catechism of the Catholic Church (CCC), thereby making it appear as though this was Christ's actual instruction. 'Purgatory's' harsh requirements are as follows:

(1) that there is a purification after death,

(2) that this purification involves pain or discomfort, and…

(3) that God assists those in this purification in response to the actions of the living.
CCC 1030-32

Notice Item (3), which dares to allege that one's time in hell is determined by the goodness or the badness of 'the living'…meaning our relatives…as though one's internment in hell hinges upon their goodness or badness in life.

Baby Hell

In December of 2005, CNN reported that the Vatican issued a statement upholding the doctrine of 'baby hell'...also known as *Limbus Infantium*...as an official Catholic doctrine.

You might remember Nicole Kidman's role as the neurotic mother in *The Others*, wherein her character tells the children, "You'll be sent to limbo if you ever deny Christ." Unfortunately, this is not fiction and happens around Catholic dinner tables every day. Kidman's character was talking about *Limbus Infantium*, which is in direct conflict with what Christ actually said about children:

Matthew 19:14

"Let the children alone, and don't stop them from coming to Me because Heaven **belongs to them."**

Several things should be noted here. Christ said children will **never** be disqualified from His presence in this life or the next. Notice that He also said Heaven "belongs to them" which means they may enter heaven **automatically** and are not required to ask for permission, unlike adults.

Even secular authorities understand that children are mentally and physiologically incapable, and therefore cannot be held accountable for anything they do. The Vatican, on the other hand, holds infants in contempt while they are yet in the womb.

As a side-note, Christ's statement also speaks to the pop-culture notion that some houses are haunted by the 'ghosts of disembodied children.'

This is not possible since Christ said they go immediately to Him at the point of death. In other words, there is no such thing in all of God's Creation as a lost child floating around in the abyss. Therefore, if it's not a child haunting the house, what is it? The only available answer is: they are evil entities masquerading as children.

2nd Corinthians 11:14

And is it any wonder, because Satan goes around disguising himself as an angel of light.

Demons know the occupants of the home are more likely to allow a 'lost child' to stay. Before long, however, the spirit shows its true colors, begins to bite and scratch the homeowners, and push them down the stairs, etc.

Mad Men

The absurd notion of *Limbus Infantium* was first promulgated into a canonized doctrine by fourth century Catholic practitioners, all of whom are identified in the Catholic Encyclopedia. Take for instance, Gregory Nazianzus (d. 389), who said:

"It will happen…that those infants dying without baptism will not be admitted by the just judge to the glory of Heaven…"

Catholic Encyclopedia [Orat. xl, 23], Limbo, II, Limbus Infantium, 1.Pre-Augustinian Tradition.

Notice that Nazianzus presumes himself to decide what happens to infants, regardless of Christ's easy provisions. Thirty years later, Augustine of Hippo Regius (354-430 A.D.) bumped it up a notch at the 418 A.D. Council of Carthage. He said:

> "All unbaptized infants must share in the common misery of the damned."
>
> Catholic Encyclopedia / Limbo / II.2. Teaching of Augustine.

It seems the doctrine took on more blood thirst as time went on. By referring to 'the damned' Augustine meant 'hell' and by 'common misery' he meant 'torment'; thereby daring to imply that infants will burn in hell, alongside those who actually deserve to be there.

Six centuries later, Pope Innocent III (1161-1216 A.D.) finally declared 'baby hell' too cruel for digestion, and diluted the doctrine to suit his more fragile sensibilities:

> "Those children dying with only original sin on their souls will suffer no other pain...except the pain of being deprived forever of the vision of God."
>
> New Advent Catholic Encyclopedia Corp. [Juris, Decret. l. III, tit. xlii, c. iii–Majores, Limbo, II. Limbus Infantium, 3. Post-Augustinian Teaching.

Although Pope Innocent's 12th Century edict on *Limbus Infantium* was kinder and gentler, by then it was too late; the damage was done. Anyone who dared speak against 'limbo' or any other Catholic fabrication was systematically hunted down and killed during the Dark Ages.

To the present day, priests and nuns around the world continue to cite 'Purgatory' as a key tool with which to frighten and control its parishioners, regardless of the kinder revision.

Now, Pope Innocent III couldn't seem to make up his mind. As a lifelong proponent of 'poena damni' (punishment of the damned), he later ordered that all infants must receive "a certain degree of spiritual torment, but in the state of perfect and natural happiness."

The question is, what 'natural happiness' can possibly be found in torment of any kind?

Sadly, the unholy doctrine of 'suffering' eventually crept into many Christian teachings as well; all of which have their sordid origins in the Holy Roman Catholic Empire.

Post Cards From Hell

The Catholic Church regularly helps itself to Old and New Testament scriptures in order to promulgate its 'Purgatory' propaganda.

Take for instance 1st Corinthians 3:13-15. The Catholic Church uses this passage of scripture as its main primer to 'prove' that 'Purgatory' exists. In this particular account, the Apostle Paul wrote a simple letter to the general assembly at the ancient city of Corinth, to alert them to the fact that Christian life could, at times, be very tough. Take a look:

Selma Kerren

1st Corinthians 3:13-15
"Each one's work will...be revealed by fire, and the fire will test each one's work, and reveal what kind it is."

Catholic practitioners ran amuck with this scripture, and peddled it as the literal 'proof of 'Purgatory.' Go to any Catholic retail shop and you will find a little postcard showing the illustration of a woman bound in chains, obediently languishing in fire. Beneath the illustration are, of course, Paul's words to the Corinthians:

The fire will test each one's work.

And that's how it goes with every scripture the Catholic Church pulls out of the hat; like pulling scripture from Genesis Chapter 3, and declaring we all have to wear fig leaves from now on.

Country Club Privileges

Now, since the doctrine of 'Purgatory' is fraught with errors, the Vatican has yet to explain what sins an infant could possibly commit, as to lock him out of Heaven forever.

Whatever the case, the old tripe apparently does not cut muster with several, modern-day popes either. In fact, two of its most recent and wildly popular popes openly defected from the doctrine. Take for instance Pope John Paul II's August 4, 1999, address to the general audience, wherein he said:

"Purgatory' **does not indicate a place** but a condition of life. Those who, after death, live in this state of purification are already immersed in **the love of Christ,** which **lifts them out of the residue of imperfection**."

Catholic World News: 'Pope Gives Good News of 'Purgatory'' August 4, 1999

Notice that the pope claims 'Purgatory' is not a 'real place' but one that occurs here on Earth. He also said Christ "lifts out" our imperfections "after death." Following through on his logic, additional purification would therefore not be necessary. It was a complete departure from the mainstream Catholic cannon, but hardly matches what priests and nuns tell Catholic families behind closed doors.

In 1984, Cardinal Joseph Ratzinger, then head of the Vatican's *Congregation for the Doctrine of the Faith*, also defected from *Limbus Infantium*, without apology.

"Limbo has **never been a defined truth** of faith. Personally, speaking...I would drop something that has always been **only a theological hypothesis**."

Timesonline.co.uk 'Irrational Belief Won't Go Out On A Limbo'

Twenty years later, Cardinal Ratzinger went on to become Pope Benedict XVI, succeeding Pope John Paul II. He again publicly denounced *Limbus Infantium* in May of 2007, as reported by CNN in December, 2005, and dissented from the Vatican's official position. These two sensible popes, having stood up against eighteen centuries of pop-tart fables, might finally have brought the Catholic Church into the best, spiritual health of its day, were it not for the pedophile-priest scandal.

It seems Catholic leaders in positions of power regularly exercise their country club privileges to reject certain doctrines, while parishioners are forced to suffer under their immense psychological strain, century after century.

The Church's Infallible Code?

Vatican officials have never satisfactorily explained these flip-flop changes concerning 'Purgatory', and how could they possibly? They cannot afford to make a single mistake!

The Vatican purports itself to be the one and only entity ever selected on Earth to hear from God. Hence, the Vatican calls itself 'The Holy See.' For this reason, everything the Vatican dictates must, at all costs, be error-free and infallible! Take a look:

> The canon law is the **church's infallible code,** and **not one dot or coma** can ever be changed. Rome and the canon law must either stand or perish altogether. Chapter VI, Canon Law

And yet, the popes of The Holy See openly defy each other. One purports, "all infants must burn in the fire," while another purports, "this has never been a defined truth." According to the Vatican's own 'law' the church must now "perish altogether."

What Legacy?

Now, Vatican officials also claim the Apostle Peter 'personally' transferred his ecclesiastical authority to the early Catholic practitioners while he was yet alive.

The Vatican purports, Peter's authority was then passed down the line, through the centuries, to the modern-day popes. It's why they call Peter *The Prince of the Apostles*. This belief is based on something that Christ said to Peter in the Book of Matthew:

Matthew 16:18
"You are Peter, and on this rock I will build My church, and the gates of Hades shall not prevail against it."

The Vatican's ignorance concerning this statement is multiple, not to mention embarrassing. First, while it is true that 'Peter' means 'rock' in Greek, it is also true that the word 'rock' was a term used in the common Aramaic and Greek languages meaning 'earth' and 'world'.

Thus, Christ did not say He would build a church exclusively around Peter...but on the Earth!

Next, there is no evidence to support that Christ named Peter the 'prince' of the Apostles. On the contrary, the exact opposite is true. According to several New Testament accounts, Peter has always been considered the 'loveable church screw-up' whose impetuous and childish behaviors leave the reader bewildered on more than one occasion.

Recall the day of the crucifixion, when bystanders asked Peter three times if he knew Jesus of Nazareth. The 'prince' of the Apostles denied it three times, and then cussed them out...fisherman style.

Even after the crucifixion, Peter's behavior hardly qualified him as a 'church boss.' One day, the Apostle Paul rode into town and noticed that Peter, along with several other dignitaries, refused to eat with new church converts because they were Gentiles. In doing so, Peter had broken Christ's strictest commandment, which was to welcome all people to the table of God...Jew and Gentile alike.

The showdown is well-recorded in Galatians 2:11-14, wherein Paul confronted Peter to the face in front of everyone, and basically read him the riot act for this hypocrisy.

As a young disciple, it is perfectly understandable why Peter fell short of the mark so many times (like we all would have done), but this time there was no excuse. He was now a commissioned Apostle and had no excuse.

Technically, Peter's actions are comparable to the white minister who turns away people at the church door...for the color of their skin.

By announcing Peter as the 'prince' of the Apostles, does the Catholic Church endorse his behavior? Most telling of all is that the 'prince' of the Apostles contributed hardly any writings to the New Testament, besides two small scrolls. Peter eventually dropped off the scene altogether, until his gruesome death some time around 65 A.D.

Paul, on the other hand, was the Johnny-come-lately ex-murderer, who wrote over two-thirds of the New Testament, opened and organized *all* the Christian churches throughout the known world at that time, trained and ordained pastors, evangelists and prophets, raised money for missionary work, stood before Emperors to present Christ, and, unlike Peter, never *once* waivered in his walk.

Nevertheless, Vatican officials continue to claim Peter as the one and only *Prince of the Apostles*. They also claim to have evidence of a first pope going back to the year 65 A.D., which happens to be around the same time Peter was killed. No doubt this was the perfect time to hijack Peter's title and begin concocting one's own stuff.

If Vatican officials insist their legacy comes from the junior and bumbling Apostle...don't try to stop them. It explains a lot.

Hearing Voices?

Now, let's assume for the moment that the Vatican's authority *did* come directly from Peter. If that is the case, there is no excuse for what happened next. After a series of historical events, the Holy Roman Catholic Empire became an official organism in the year 380 A.D. Over the next thousand years, the entire continent of Europe found itself in the Vatican's death-grip, known as The Dark Ages.

During this era, several depraved doctrines emerged from The Holy See, which are highly prohibited in Bible scripture. Each item includes the Bible reference forbidding the practice.

> Commanding priests to abstain from marriage   1st Timothy 4:1-4

> Teaching that marital-sex is sinful, if enjoyed for pleasure
Hebrews 13:4

> Teaching that deadly diseases are 'blessings' from God
Isaiah 5:1-5 / Acts 10:38 / 1 Peter 2:24

> Forcing vows of poverty; that poverty is a 'gift' of God
Ecclesiastes 10:19 & 7:12 / 2nd Corinthians 9:8

> Paying Indulgences (heaven's cover charge)
Ephesians 2:8 / 1st Corinthians 5:11

> Praying to wooden and plastic statues of dead people
Leviticus 26:1

> Making Mary a goddess ('The Queen of Heaven')
John 14:6 / Leviticus 26:1

> Repetitive chanting over rosary beads   Matthew 6:7

> Excessive secrecy and obstructing investigations
1st Timothy 5:20-21 / Ephesians 5:11-13

> Plastering gargoyles (demon dogs) on church buildings
1st Thessalonians 5:22 / 2nd Corinthians 6:15

> Worshiping Christ still nailed to the cross   Luke 24:5-6

> Teaching 'Purgatory' and *Limbus Infantium*
Galatians 1:8-9 / Luke 23:43

> Flagellation (beating and mutilating oneself to gain 'favor'
from God)   Philippians 3:2

> Confiscating the written Testaments from world-view for
twelve hundred years.   Mark 16:15

Who gave The Holy See permission to enforce these practices? Was it hearing voices? The most depraved of these teachings is perhaps that deadly diseases are 'a blessing' from God. Seeing these hellish propensities coming during his own life time, the Apostle Paul said:

Galatians 1:6-9
Some are trying to harass you, and pervert the Good News. If anyone comes along and preaches any other Good News than the one we brought you, he is cursed. Again, he is cursed!

Philippians 4:2
Beware of dogs, beware of evil workers, beware of the practice of mutilation.

Paul challenged these infiltrators on their own illogic. If they were so hell-bent on flagellation in order to gain favor from God, why stop at nicks and scratches? Why not go all the way, and make the cut where it counts? That shut them up for a while...at least while Paul was alive.

Massive Cover-Up

About forty years after Christ's crucifixion, Emperor Titus of Rome marched on Judea and sacked it in the year 70 A.D. All collaboration on the Testaments came to a temporary halt as the Jews fled to every corner of the known world. They would not return to Israel until 1948. Although Christ commanded that all mankind be allowed to hear the Good News of the Gospel, (specifically, that gruesome religious requirements had finally come to an end) the newly formed Catholic Church seized upon the lull, confiscated both Testaments around 380 A.D., and hid them from world view for over twelve-hundred years.

In 382 A.D., the Catholic Church commissioned a monk, named Jerome, to translate both Testaments into Latin, considered to be the rich man's language. Knowing perfectly well that no poor commoner would ever be able to understand the Latin texts, the breach between God and man was now complete.

Predictably, the Latin document that emerged was littered with outrageous manipulations. Known as the Vulgate (meaning 'vulgar') the Catholic Church insists to this day that theirs is the only true Bible. For this reason, Catholic retailers stock only the Catholic Bible and never "that other one."

During the Dark Ages, anyone within the Vatican's reach found in possession of either Testaments in any other language but Latin, was systematically interrogated and put to death.

According to documents found all over Europe, scholars today believe that upwards of two million persons were tortured and killed by the Vatican during this time, for any number of reasons, like: being Jewish, possessing another translation, questioning the Vatican's rogue doctrines, dabbling in scientific explorations, and so forth.

The Vatican's murder spree ran amuck until the early 1800s, when the world finally had enough. Till then, no matter what crimes the Vatican committed, the first order of business was to protect 'Mother Church' as evidenced by the oath every priest must take:

"I, _____, (priest, bishop, cardinal) of the Holy Roman Church, promise and swear to…keep secret [anything that] could cause damage or dishonor to the Holy Church…So help me Almighty God."

The Vatican writhes in secrecy because of this self-imposed internal policy, and again defies the true instructions of the Apostles concerning church crimes and perversions. Take a look:

1st Corinthians 5:11-13
Do not keep company with any [Christian] brother engaged in [perversions]…do not even eat with someone like that…Expel that evil one from among you…

1st Timothy 5:20
Those in authority who are sinning, rebuke them in front of everyone, so that all may fear.

Matthew 18:17
If your brother refuses to hear about his offense, bring him up before the entire church. If he still refuses, treat him as you would an evil doer.

Notice that these instructions do not apply to people outside the church, but specifically to 'seasoned' Christians and church leaders. Now, apply the above instructions to the pedophile priest epidemic and you'll see, first hand, the Vatican's utter failure to engage in the protection its own parishioners. In each instance, we see that secret sins perpetrated by clergy of any cloth should **never be covered up.** Rather, they are to be exposed and stopped from thriving, otherwise they will gain power and spread.

Ephesians 5:11-12
Have nothing to do with the evil activities hidden
in darkness; rather, expose them with bright light,
so that it cannot continue.

Today, Catholic practitioners can no longer hide the larvae of its modern-day pedophile-priest scandal, and finds itself paying victims in excess of $1 Billion, despite its useless secret oaths.

The Malleus Maleficarum

In the year 1440 Johann Gutenberg of Germany invented the printing press. With the New Testament printed one page at a time, commoners all over Europe finally read the true words of Christ for the first time in their lives, in their own simple languages. Happy riots broke out all over Europe outside printing shops, as they brawled for more pages of the New Testament.

From there things quickly spun out of control as one hot question after another mounted against the Vatican, and its foul doctrines. Free thinkers of the day, such as Englishmen John

Wycliffe, William Tyndale, and the German monk, Martin Luther, challenged the Vatican on its bastardized doctrines.

Several European royals also entered the fray, such as the English Protestant Kings, James and Henry VIII, and Queen Elizabeth I; and the German Lord Frederick of Saxony; but they could only provide nominal protection for the Protestants.

By the late 1400s, the Protestant Movement was well underway, but not without untold bloodshed. Vatican inquisitors scoured the countryside for Protestant defectors, and harangued them with relentless inquisitions, which soon escalated to torture and public burnings at the stake all over Europe.

Great Britain's John Foxe (1516-1587) compiled eyewitness accounts of these tortures in his rather large, volume entitled, *Foxe's Book of Martyrs,* the contents of which are the most heartbreaking and reprehensible in all of human history.

John Foxe recorded that male and female victims alike were dragged in, and stripped naked before large audiences of state and clergy officials, in order to punish them for their 'heresy.'

Hysterically, the torture always began with the ceremonial, spread-eagle, shaving of pubic hair before everyone in the room, followed by a litany of excruciating torture directed at the victims' genitals and rectums.

Considering its chaste and virginal representation, the Vatican has yet to explain what exposed genitals and rectums have to do with cleansing 'heretics' of their sins. The acts prove the Catholic Church's early predilection for perversions.

And then, just in time for Christmas, Pope Innocent VIII issued a handy-dandy torture manual on December 5, 1484, called the *Malleus Maleficarum* (meaning 'witch hammer'). The *Maleficarum* came complete with a written set of instructions on shaving the victim's pubic hair, how often they should be tortured, and what flesh-tearing instrument to use. Below are choice excerpts from the *Maleficarum* demonstrating the full impact of the atrocities. From the 1928 Montague Summers translation:

> The third instruction is that the hair should be shaved from every part of her body, because they hide superstitious objects in their clothes and even inside the most secret parts of their bodies, which should not be named here...At the slightest torture they admit everything, even some things which are not true...especially if they have been tortured before, even if their arms are only slightly twisted...And while she is bound [naked] and raised from the ground, let the Judge read her again the accusations...Finally, if she will not admit to her crimes, he should ask her if she is ready to endure the ordeal by red-hot iron.
>
> Excerpts from Malleus Maleficarum, Part 3, Questions XIV, XV and XVI.

Many Catholics contend the *Maleficarum* was a rogue document that was never approved by the Vatican, but it's a little too late for that defense. In a letter dispatched throughout the Holy Roman Empire, dated December 9, 1484, Pope Innocent VIII endorsed the document wholeheartedly and by it, gave his inquisitors unlimited power to steal, kill and destroy. Take a look:

"We grant permission to the Inquisitor…to proceed, according to the regulations of the Inquisition, against every person no matter their rank…with excommunication…and yet more terrible penalties, censures, and punishment, as may seem good to him…as often as he wishes."

License To Kill

Now let's examine some other official documents. Accumulated over the centuries, the Catholic Canon Law is the litany of written regulations by which the Vatican governs itself. Speaking specifically against accused heretics, the Canon Law gave itself the unmitigated license to kill.

It is commanded that archbishops…once or twice every year inquire for heretics…This goodly work of purgation is to be conducted in the following manner:

I. Excommunication. This sentence is to be pronounced on notorious heretics, those suspected of heresy, those who harbor, defend, or assist them, or who [talk], trade, and communicate with them.

II. Proscription: (the process of humiliation) From all offices, ecclesiastical or civil, from all public duties and private rights.

III. Confiscation: Of all their personal belongings and real estate.

IV. Death: The last punishment is DEATH; sometimes by the sword,--more commonly by fire.

Jus Canonicum; Digestum et Enucleatum juxta Ordinem Librorum et Titulorum qui in Decretalibus Epistolis Gregorii IX. P. M. Georgii Adami Struvi, pp. 359-363: Lipsiae et Jenae, 1688.

Unmistakably, Item III explains how the Vatican amassed its great wealth...**by killing and stealing** the properties of its victims, while Item IV instructs the inquisitor to burn the victims at the stake. Another document now hidden from worldview is the decree granting full pardon to inquisitors who murdered on behalf of the Vatican:

> "These acts should not be considered homicides, if the inquisitor, for zeal of Mother Church, happens to kill excommunicated persons." Decreti, pars ii, causa xxiii, quaest v. can, xlvii.

The Vatican has no possible way of denying its long-standing approval of torture and murder, as long as these writings are forever obtainable by the viewing public. And how could it possibly explain them? It doesn't make mistakes, remember? The Vatican then makes another flip-flop change against its own written laws with this 20th Century edict, as though God were the one who 'changed his mind' about killing people.

> "...Terrorism which threatens, wounds, kills, [and] tortures...to extract confession...is contrary to respect for the person and for human dignity." Church Catechism No. 2297.

OK, so which is it? Does the 'Mother Church' condone or condemn murder on its behalf? Whatever the case, the Canon Law defies the New Testament, which clearly states:

1ˢᵗ John 3:15
"Whoever hates his **brother** is a murderer, and no murderer has eternal life abiding in him."

It appears that murderers on death-row stand a better chance of entering Heaven, than zealots who murder over religion.

The Cutlery Set

Instruments used on victims in the Dark Ages were sharp, terrifying, flesh-tearing products, specifically designed to elicit 'confessions' on sight. Eyewitness sketches of the instruments used by Vatican and state officials can be viewed on the following website, and is not for the faint of heart. Page down a few clicks and the images become more terrifying:

http://www.bibliotecapleyades.net/vatican/esp_vatican29.htm

The Catholic Church denies that it was ever involved in the extermination of 'heretics' at any time. When we questioned clerics via telephone at the Los Angeles Diocese, one answered, "Well, that's the way things were done back in those days."

But it was not the way Christ said to do it!

59

Another cleric said, "Well, only about three-thousand people were killed during the inquisitions, not millions like secular historians suggest."

Another challenged, "Well, it wasn't just the Catholic Church. What about the Salem witch trials perpetrated by Christians?"

Yes, and what about them? Whereas the pilgrims of Salem, 1692, tried to escape religious tyranny by fleeing to the New World, they could not escape the predilections they learned from their former abusers.

The St. Bartholomew's Day Massacre

The Los Angeles Diocese's claim that "only three-thousand" perished at the hands of the Vatican during the Dark Ages is completely discredited by secular, public records all over Europe.

By the year 1572, France was fully engulfed in the Catholic-Protestant War, as was the rest of Europe. (The Vatican just couldn't let go!)

Then, Pope Gregory XIII came along and stuck his pious finger into French King Henry's face, and condemned his lusty antics at court. The pope threatened to deny the king "entry to Heaven" (as though he had the right to make that decision), and made the king a deal that he couldn't refuse. He promised the king "absolution" if he were to "kill every Protestant in France."

Severely convicted by his own sins, the ignorant king took the deal. King Henry dispatched invitations to all the Huguenots (French Protestants) all over the country, and asked them to come to a kiss-and-make-up picnic.

The event was to take place in the heart of downtown Paris. After years of fighting with the Vatican, the Huguenots arrived happily and unarmed on August 24, 1572, thinking they would finally be reconciled to their king, and live in peace. The king's soldiers, however, paired up with Vatican assassins, launched an unexpected attack against the people and slaughtered them all.

That day, over 3,000 unarmed French citizens died under the Vatican's sword, including men, women, children, and the elderly, with an additional 70,000 killed throughout the French provinces leading up to October of that year.

Hysterically, the Vatican denies any involvement in the incident to this day, but it's a little too late for that. Shortly after the massacre, the glutinous Pope Gregory XIII commissioned artists to memorialize "the blessed event" with two artifacts.

The first was a large, painted mural depicting the slaughter, by the Italian artist, Vasari, on the Vatican wall near its entrance, which is still there today. The second artifact was the Pope's literal stamp of approval, in the form of a coin, bearing his face on one side, and slain French citizens on the other. And that was just one of the massacres. There were more.

Today's Catholic Encyclopedia, *The New Advent*, calls eye-witness accounts of this massacre "the product of over-zealous protestants." If that is the case, the Vatican should hire a local painter to remove the mural from its entrance. To view the mural in question, visit:

http://www.reformation.org/bart.html.

E-Z Terms at Last

At last, we come full circle back to the subject of 'Purgatory.' The point of this exercise was to examine the full body of Catholic bastardizations and match them against true Christian teaching.

Now let's examine what Christ and the Apostles really said about our entry to Heaven.

Ephesians 2:8-9

You have been saved through God's gracious invitation, by simply believing. **It's a free gift** from God, and has nothing to do with working for it, in case anyone wants to boast about how 'good' he is.

Romans 10:13

Whoever calls on the Lord will be rescued.

Colossians 2:14

Christ has wiped out the list of requirements against us, took it out of the way, and nailed it to the cross.

When closely scrutinized, the hellish doctrine of 'Purgatory', and its bi-product of torture, quickly disintegrates before our eyes. Much of the world still suffers today because of the tremors of the Roman Catholic Church, especially in the areas of guilt and punishment. And yet, whenever disaster strikes somewhere in the world, media personalities can't run fast enough for commentary from Catholic officials with their starchy, white collars. But why should they look for answers from an institution that has hurt the world so badly, and for so long?

Is it any wonder that mankind groped for ways to free itself from religion? When the *Theory of Evolution* came along, it must have seemed like winning the Lotto!

God has been trying to tell us for a very long time that Christ's crucifixion brought an end to cruel, religious rituals. Messages from Heaven, however, are all too often drowned out by the pounding of tyranny.

Clearly, the doctrine of 'Purgatory' is a complete fraud. The people of the Catholic Church deserve better than this, and so does the world.

Myth 5

The Jews.

Did They Really

Kill Christ?

While it is true that those who killed Christ were Jewish, it is **not true** that the whole nation of Jews was involved. In fact, the exact opposite is true.

This particular discussion merits a closer look since countless Jews in past times were **killed** over the allegation. Therefore, preachers might want to think before they speak on the matter.

It's been a highly charged topic for many centuries, one that is laced with racist undertones, whose roots sink down into the most surprising caverns of dark, religious thought.

For instance, shocking are the handwritten, venomous notations of Protestant heroes, Martin Luther and John Calvin:

> "Such a desperate, evil, poisonous and devilish lot are these Jews...it all coincides with the judgment of Christ, which declares they are venomous, bitter, vindictive, tricky serpents, assassins, and children of the devil..."
>
> On the Jews and Their Lies, Luther's Works, Volume 47.

> "[The Jews] are rotten, unbending and stubborn people who deserve unending oppression without measure, and they should die in their misery without the pity of anyone."
>
> Excerpt from "Ad Quaelstiones et Objecta Juaei Cuiusdam Responsio" by John Calvin.

Is it possible that the most esteemed Protestants, who fought daily against religious tyranny, harbored such hatred for a race of people? Too bad they were all wrong, as you will soon discover.

Next, is an excerpt from Chapter 3 of the Vatican's *Malleus Maleficarum*, which displays the Vatican's actual instructions to exterminate the Jews:

> "Besides, in the last Canon Law concerning Jews it says: his goods are to be confiscated, and he is to be condemned to death, because with perverse doctrine he opposed the Faith of Christ..."

Notice that the *Maleficarum* cites the Canon Law; the regulatory body of text by which the Vatican governs itself. Let's do a quick side-by-side comparison of the true words of Christ and the Catholic Canon Law:

Christ said:

"If anyone hears My words and does not keep them, I do not judge that person; for I have not come into the world to judge, but to save them."

John 12:47

But the Vatican said:

"The Jew is to be condemned to death, because with perverse doctrine he opposed the faith of Christ…"

So, let's get this straight. Christ said, if anyone rejected Him, He refused to judge them; but the Vatican took it upon itself to "put them to death" for rejecting Him? Again, who gave them permission to do that?

Although the above excerpts reflect extremist views, they actually mirror denominational church thinking, to a greater or lesser degree. The Protestants' confusion stems from several events recorded in the New Testament, wherein Christ pointed His finger at two specific, Jewish groups, known as the Pharisees and Sadducees. He denounced them publicly, and called them "a brood of vipers" and "children of your father, the devil."

The Pharisees and Sadducees, about three hundred in number at the Temple Jerusalem, were the administrative leaders, and über-religious hypocrites of the day, who went about masquerading as 'holy men'; when in fact, they were embezzlers of the national welfare fund, exploiters of the temple, and abusers of the poor and elderly.

Upon closer inspection of the actual events, it turns out that Christ **never once condemned a Jewish commoner**...that working class man whom He rescued, defended and healed day after day. No, at all times, He condemned the corrupt, religious leaders, not the ordinary commoner; and there was a large, honking difference between the two!

As a result of this obfuscation, public speculation has run amuck over the centuries, countless Jews lost their lives, and the true identity of Christ's killers is buried forever. Or is it?

The Line-Up

The true identity of conspirators is no secret, and never was. New Testament records consistently point to one, small group, and leaves no question as to their identity. That group is identified again and again as:

1. Ciaphas, the appointed high priest of that year

2. The chief priests under Ciaphas (about 200)

3. And the elders (72)

This brings us to a sub-total of 273. The New Testament collectively refers to this petite group as, sometimes the Elders, sometimes the Sanhedrin, but mostly as the Council. The Council was comprised to two sects of scholar: the Sadducees and Pharisees.

The Council held high court over the religious, commercial, and judicial affairs of all Israel, from offices located within the Great Temple at Jerusalem.

It's a well-known fact among clergy members that the true killers of Christ was the Council, and not the Jewish commoners, but it's a delineation that today's clergy refuses to make; perhaps for the simple reason that harboring prejudice against the Jews is a delicious seduction that zealots cannot do without.

This chapter presents evidence that only a **small handful** of conspirators were involved in the crucifixion of Christ.

Furthermore, Hollywood films and Sunday morning preachers both describe the whole nation of Jews as condemning Christ to death, and yet, the evidence proves nothing of the sort is true.

We all saw the 2002 interview with Diane Sawyer and Mel Gibson, concerning his movie, *The Passion of the Christ*. Attempting to enflame the controversy, Sawyer pressed Gibson to identify those who killed Jesus. She wanted him to say it was the Jews. Instead, he answered, "I killed Him. It was my sins that nailed Him to the cross."

Although Gibson's humility was surprising, his answer was incorrect. There is an answer far more naked and true found in the New Testament.

Christ walked Himself to the cross

Without help from anyone!

The Chamber of Commerce

As a conquered nation, Israel's economy was impossibly strained during the first century by Rome's heavy tax demands. Wage rations for temple personnel were derived from meager donations, known as 'tithes' collected from commoners who suffered even more under Rome's tax grip.

Add on payroll for scribes, guards, personal assistants, and a corrupt welfare system, it is reasonable to assume that only a limited number of personnel could have been employed in the Temple Jerusalem at any given time. In that day, there simply wasn't the purse for more.

Furthermore, the New Testament record of Luke Chapter 7 shows that many of the Jewish districts were, in fact, so strained, they relied upon Roman benevolence to build their temples. To the Jewish palate, this must have seemed like *eating pork*.

Their dire financial straits, however, left them no choice but to take the handouts. Now, to subsidize its strained economy, the Council eventually sunk to a new kind of depth, not seen in Israel since its saucy, idolatrous days before the Babylon Invasion.

The Council permitted merchants to buy, sell and trade goods of every kind inside the temple!

To any garden-variety, infernal prophet of Israel, this was enough to set his hair on fire. Days before His crucifixion, Jesus of Nazareth became unhinged at the sight of this exploitation inside the temple, picked up a leather strap, and whipped the place to shreds.

Now, despite its battered state of affairs, the Council took its power very seriously, in the parsimonious sense, and frowned upon any young upstart who rode into town, stirring things up. The Council's contention with one Jesus of Nazareth began the first day it laid eyes on Him, and soon escalated into three, bold-faced assassination attempts.

But how would the Council members possibly accomplish this? If they harmed Jesus in front of commoners, riots would have broken out all over Judea, and they knew it.

Jesus Christ, Super Star

From the very start of His work on Earth, Jesus was the most controversial and sought-after Prophet in world history. Hordes ran after Him, pressed Him on every side, and trampled one another just to touch His clothing.

In one case, the crowd dismantled a man's roof just to get to Him. Imagine sitting in your living-room with distinguished guests, when suddenly people are hacking away at your ceiling. The pattern throughout the New Testament is unmistakable:

Not commoner wanted Jesus dead ... EVER!

Not one farmer, not one housewife, no butcher, baker, or candlestick maker. No one ever wanted Him dead…and why would they?

They had better use of Him alive than dead!

He brought their dead children back to life, healed their sick relatives, got prostitutes off the street, cleaned up their lepers and brought them back home, and all with instant, same-day service.

The truth is … the everyday Jew loved Jesus!

And yet, preachers and movie directors everywhere peddle the idea that the Jews who loved Jesus on Wednesday…wanted Him dead on Friday.

It's a claim that is simply not based on facts. While, it is true that many Jewish commoners regularly engaged Jesus in heated, public discussions, they adored Him to the very end.

Take for instance the event known around the world as 'Palm Sunday' (which, actually occurred on or about Tuesday). Knowing He would be crucified at Jerusalem in a matter of days, Jesus rode into the city on a donkey. When the commoners saw Him, they ran out in droves; dancing, singing and waving palm branches. And they threw their clothing on the ground for His donkey to trample on.

Jesus was well over three years into His work by that time and every household in Israel was **irreversibly affected** by Him. In other words, crowd-control had become impossible. Take a look:

Matthew 21:8-11

A large multitude spread their cloaks on the road shouting, 'Hosanna!'…the **whole city** was stirred up…

Mark 2:1-5

Jesus entered Capernaum…there was **no room left**, not even outside…so they dismantled the roof and let down a paralytic on his cot.

Mark 3:9

He instructed the disciples to keep a small boat ready for Him in case the **crowd crushed Him.**

Luke 12:1

Meanwhile, a crowd of many thousands had gathered, and were **trampling** on one another …

Doing the Math

The petite number of conspirators who wanted Jesus dead is now much clearer to see. The high priest and his cohorts comprised about three hundred.

Let's mix in two hundred temple guards, and the odd five-hundred angry merchants, whose product tables Jesus overturned, and we clock in at a cool thousand. But wait, there's more!

To be generous, let's throw in another two hundred visiting priests from minor synagogues, who might have heard about the

Jesus controversy, and the final tally brings us to twelve-hundred conspirators; not an unreasonable sum. However, that twelve hundred was also subjected to serious, daily assault. New Testament records prove defectors of every rank and file abandoned the Council in favor of Jesus, based on the miracles they saw Him do. Within the Apostle John's hearing, one priest admitted they were licked:

John 12:19
"You see? We have accomplished nothing. The whole world has gone after Him."

By 'whole world' the Council member meant 'all of Israel.' This now brings us full circle back to the main point of the discussion. Hence, the depiction of 'thousands' shouting *Crucify him! Crucify him!* in Hollywood films is nowhere near the true number.

In fact, the Council's membership was so crumbled, it sought also to assassinate Jewish commoners whom Jesus healed, because their in-your-face testimony became a daily humiliation.

John 12:9-11
But the chief priests plotted to kill Lazarus also, because on account of him, many of the Jews went away after Jesus.

After being dead four days, Jesus raised Lazarus from the dead, and the man came out from a death-tomb in front of the whole city wrapped in grave cloths. After that, the daily defections sealed the Council's defeat.

Christ's massive appeal meant the conspirators could never have hovered above four or five hundred at a time, and frankly, even that number is flamboyant. Critics of the Jews have yet to reconcile how this petite group equates to an entire nation. And yet, this group had all the power and connections to Rome, and could spin any tale they liked.

Black Ops

The Council shows up with a lot of bravado on every page of the Gospels to harangue the young Prophet on the preaching circuit. They questioned His authority, called Him a bastard, drunkard, demoniac, and fraud.

The actual abduction of Jesus, however, would be another matter all together. It was an ambitious undertaking that would require swift execution, the cover of night, and without the people's knowledge. The next exhibit was recorded by a priest-defector named Nicodemus, and gives us a glimpse into the actual abduction.

Mark 14:1-2

On the Passover, the Council plotted to arrest Him
by trickery and kill Him. But they said, "Not during
the Passover, in case the people start a riot."

Notice the word 'riot.' As any black ops agent will tell you, conspiracies of this magnitude cannot be kept under wraps for long, especially if the rioters involve an entire city. There's always a press leak, or a disgruntled cabinet aide, an overlooked employee, or someone who wants to stick it to the man. It was no different in first century Jerusalem.

The temple doorman would have told the scullery maid, and she would have told her lover, the blacksmith. The blacksmith would have called his cousins, and they would have run into all the neighborhoods, pounding on doors. The shop owner, whose kid brother got healed by Jesus, would have woken up his brothers and uncles, and the old woman, whose son was cleansed of leprosy, would have rounded up the men-folk in her family, so on and so forth.

Within the hour, riots would have broken out all over the city, scrapping the entire crucifixion. This is why the Council had to arrest Jesus in the middle of the night and without the people's knowledge…because they were woefully out-numbered. But then, in the early hours of one frosty, April morning they finally got Him.

Mark 15:1
Immediately that morning, the chief priests, elders
and council conspired together, bound Jesus, and
delivered Him to the Roman governor.

After Jesus' arrest, the Council attempted to incite Jewish commoners to testify against Him, but the barrio, if you please, closed ranks and refused to cooperate.

Mark 14:55

The chief priests and all the counsel sought testimony against Jesus to put Him to death, but they couldn't find anyone to do it.

Notice that the Jewish commoners sought to protect Him, not kill Him. Although the New Testament states several times that 'the multitude' came to arrest Him, there was no commoner among them. Take a look:

Matthew 26:47

And behold, Judas, came with a great multitude carrying swords and clubs, **from the chief priests and elders** of the people, and he kissed Jesus...

The arresting party came **"from the chief priests."** It is appalling that the 17th century Bible translators failed to properly articulate the difference between Council and commoner. If the two groups were one and the same, there would be no reason to arrest Him at night.

The truth is, the good people of Jerusalem were all tucked away in their beds, asleep; exactly where they were supposed to be in the middle of the night. Furthermore, it was Passover, which meant they were not allowed to be out and about doing anything! So perfect was the opportunity to execute Him.

No doubt Judas Iscariot kept it a secret, at least for twenty-four hours. For one year's wages, just about anyone would keep their mouth shut...and kiss you on the cheek to boot.

Death by Cop

With our attention now focused on the true killers, the Council's so-called power comes into question. Was this group of religious leaders really strong enough to overpower Christ? Or, did He go along with their plan willingly? Of their power, Jesus said:

> John 10: 18
> "No one can take My life away from Me. I lay it down by Myself. I have the power to lay it down and the power to bring Myself back to life again…"

When we examine the words, movements and actions of Jesus of Nazareth during His last days, an unmistakable pattern emerges, as though He was the very **architect** of His own crucifixion. He knew precisely where the crucifixion was to take place, and told the disciples the location well ahead of time.

It was in Jerusalem where His miracles were most hotly scrutinized. Jerusalem was the only place in all the Middle East where He was in any kind of danger at all, and yet He walked straight into the trap.

> Luke 9:51
> Now when the time had come for Him to be crucified, He set His face toward Jerusalem with unwavering conviction.

The Council did not force him to go there, nor did the Romans. He could easily have by passed Jerusalem altogether, and fled to any number of regions; a point which Mel Gibson articulated in several of his interviews. There was no Interpol in those days, no fugitive network, or satellite tracking system. The world was a very large place to get lost in. He could have traveled to Britannia, Germania, Gaul, Egypt, or Mesopotamia, never to be seen or heard from again. Instead, He walked straight into His own death.

Upon Jesus' arrival at Jerusalem, the next event is both puzzling and tragic. Instead of keeping a low profile to delay his imminent execution, He walked straight into the Great Temple, picked up yet another leather strap, and again proceeded to whip the place to shreds. It was the final act that rang the dinner bell for the Council, and basically invited them to bring it on.

It would not be the first or last time in history that a man, condemned to death, threw down the gauntlet, all or nothing.

The Council arrested Jesus the following dawn. Standing inside the Praetorium before Pontius Pilate at about 8:00 A.M., He was read the official charge of treason, punishable by death.

Interesting to note is that the governor knew Jesus was innocent and tried to release Him **three times**, but He refused to cooperate in the matter of His own release.

John 19:10

Pilate said to Him, "What are you doing? Are you trying to ignore me? Don't you know I have the power to crucify you, or release you?"

Meantime, the Council, standing outside the gate, incited the crowd to shout *Crucify him! Crucify him!*

No doubt this crowd was the sordid mixture of temple supporters, merchants, and out-of-towners, whose tables Jesus overturned in the temple; and they were only too happy to get rid if Him. And Jesus, not wishing to keep them waiting any longer took off the gloves.

John 18:37

Pilate asked Him if He claimed to be a king, and He replied, "Yes, that's correct. I am a King. And this is the reason why I came into the world. This is what My father has asked Me to do."

At that moment, the Roman and the Galilean understood one another perfectly. By claiming to be a king, Jesus had committed treason against the Emperor of Rome. Considering the manner of execution, when was the last time we saw someone deliberately malign their own release?

The collective words, actions and movements of Jesus in the days leading up to his crucifixion become more suspect at every turn of the page. Scattered throughout the four Gospels, they tend to lose their relative thread, but paste them all together on a storyboard, and the incontrovertible pattern emerges.

John Douglas, founder of the FBI's Profiler Unit, might call it 'death by cop'. According to the basic standards of forensic psychiatry, Jesus was a man on a mission to die.

The Mixing Bowl

It has been suggested in secular and Christian circles that Adolf Hitler's World War II extermination of the Jews was 'just desserts because they killed Christ,' but this is no longer a valid argument, because the evidence proves that only the petite group of religious leaders were involved.

The translators should have been more careful in articulating who did what, as should film directors and Sunday morning preachers. Instead, the true killers and commoners are flagrantly mixed together in the same mixing bowl, until one can hardly tell them apart. And yet, every time the distinction is blurred, it could cost another Jew his or her life.

Today, most Jews are appalled by the very mention of Jesus because of the untold persecution they suffered surrounding His controversy. Sadly, it could be a breach that might never be repaired.

Fade to Black

At about nine o'clock that morning, the common folks of Jerusalem awoke to the Passover. Instead of finding holy reverence on somber streets, they were met with the rustle and crunch of an impending execution, but they didn't know whose.

Word spread quickly, just as the Council predicted. When they came out of their dwellings, the Jewish commoners saw Jesus…the Healer…stumbling about on the cobblestones, hurt and bleeding; and that's when they all cried out.

Luke 23:27
And a great multitude of the people followed Him,
along with many mourning women…

The commoners that day were understandably shaken, and too afraid to act. It's one thing to throw down a riot inside a Jewish temple, but a whole other matter to pick a street-fight with Rome.

By all appearances, the Romans had arrested Jesus, because they were the ones now whipping Him about the head. However, we must understand that Jesus was the architect of His own execution, and He played the Council like a fiddle.

As it is written, He walked to the cross to pay for every sin we would ever commit.

The Council was, of course, overjoyed. Short of cocktails and party hats, the petite group followed along smugly. Why, it all fell together like a tragic Greek play. Fade to black, with the truth buried forever.

Christ's hot popularity made it tactically and logistically impossible to hide the execution plot longer than an hour. Not more than three or four hundred could possibly have been involved in His death because of the daily defections, which hardly equates to an entire nation. And yet, countless Jews were persecuted over this very allegation.

The Jews who loved Jesus on Wednesday were **not the same ones** who killed Him on Friday. Anyone who says so is woefully misguided.

Myth 6

Do All Things

Really Happen For A Reason?

This one sounds 'holy' and is actually a favorite among religions all over the world.

Until you step off the curb and get hit by a bus.

Although Christendom believes this to be the Gospel truth, it's actually a statement that cannot be found anywhere in either Testaments. Furthermore, when people say this, they lump incredibly evil things into the mix.

For instance, a man gets fired from his job and tells everyone, "Well, all things happen for a reason." But without an income, he cannot pay his bills and soon his car is repossessed.

Meantime, down the street, a family's house burns to the ground in the middle of the night and they lose everything. The mother tells the reporter, "Well, all things happen for a reason, so we're just gonna' hold on tight," but she never will find out what that reason is.

Contrary to what we have been taught, the New Testament states…"Only good and perfect things come from God above." Therefore, if you have been visited by personal tragedy, you are not obligated to receive this counsel.

For instance, should we tell the parents of a murdered child, "All things happen for a reason"?

Your response is, "Well, nobody would **ever** tell them that."

And our reply is, "Yes but, people keep saying **ALL** things happen for a reason!"

Perhaps it's time to start a world-wide campaign and modify this to, "Some things happen only to rip your heart out."

It Wasn't Meant To Be?

How did this fabrication ever get started? By now, it is practically impossible to pry it from the collective conscience of man.

Every year in January, we all look forward to *American Idol,* and the never-ending stream of hilarious contestants who provide us with weeks of laughter. The show keeps us company through our harsh, American winters, and provides us with tons of office gossip the morning after.

In the winter of 2006, a certain teenage girl showed up to audition. With long, flowing hair, literally down to her knees, she stood before the metro-hip judges, wearing an odd, Mormon-style dress; the kind that *Sister Wives* wear. Also painfully obvious was that she came from an old-church family. One tried not to laugh as she stood there, so odd and out of place.

But then she started singing. She delivered an old, church hymn with surprising soul and power. Straight down the line, all three judges said they loved her voice, but felt she didn't fit the pop-idol image the show was looking for, and they gave her the 'big no.'

She thanked the judges graciously, and ran out of the room where she fell into her father's arms, waiting outside the door. Predictably, her father was an elderly gentleman who looked to be around seventy. As she sobbed into his shoulder, the microphone picked up what she said.

"It wasn't meant to be, it just wasn't meant to be." And her father agreed. "Yes, that's right, it wasn't meant to be."

OK, so where is it etched in stone that a young person with such a gift should be stricken from opportunity on her first try? If every inventor, explorer, scientist, industrialist, artist, and entrepreneur subjected their talents to this notion, we would still be living in the Stone Age.

Sadly, the young singer was a product of the old-church nonsense. She had been taught that all things happen for a reason. Who knows if she will engage her gift ever again?

This adage is a destiny-cruncher that should be challenged head-on.

Lost In Translation

Misconceptions concerning this teaching began with a letter the Apostle Paul wrote to the assembly in Rome, around 45 A.D.

Romans 8:28
And we know that everything works together for good, toward those who love God, and have been **predestined** for His purpose.

Here, the Apostle simply tried to point out that God will help us through every hardship that **LIFE** throws at us. Notice, he did not say God actually 'sends' the hardship. And yet, church leaders use this scripture to 'prove' that God 'predestines' tragedies upon us for 'a purpose.'

The result is utter confusion. People around the world will tell you they never figured out the elusive reason for the tragedies that visited upon them. By teaching this to the public at large, church leaders dare to insinuate that evil is a necessary component for our spiritual growth. If this conjecture were true, Christ would never have prayed for evil to be kept away from us. Take a look:

Matthew 6:13
And lead us not into testing, but rescue us from evil…
Original Greek Text

Therefore, if God **rescues** us from evil, it can no longer be considered a necessary component for spiritual growth.

Upstairs-Downstairs

The 'all things happen for a reason' adage was also the church teaching that ignited the class system between the rich and poor. The 'upstairs-downstairs' line of thinking was chiseled to perfection during the Industrial Age, and saturates much of today's lust for fame and materials.

As a result, many of today's rich and famous are convinced they were predestined by God for fortune and fame, but this misconception is far from the truth.

The Judeo-Christian God never predestines one person for wealth, and another for poverty, one for health, and another for sickness; so on and so forth. He is legendary for harboring no favorites of any kind, and according to His own statements, wishes only peace, health, prosperity toward ALL mankind.

Cutting Through The Muck

Do all things happen for a reason? Well, that depends on what it is. Did it cause you mental, physical, or emotional suffering? Are you the victim of a violent crime? Where you diagnosed with a deadly disease? Did you suffer abuse at the hands of a parent or spouse? Were you born into an unstable environment that made it virtually impossible for you to get ahead in life?

If you answered 'yes' to any of these questions, rest assured that none of those events were dispatched by the Judeo-Christian God. Let's take another look:

James 1:16-17

Do not be **deceived**, beloved. Every good and perfect gift is from above…from the Father of Lights, and in Him is **no variation**, nor slightest degree of change.

Notice that the Apostle used the word 'deceived' in regards to those who believe and/or teach that evil comes from Heaven.

The Fiery Redhead

Now, let's talk about a true story involving young Mike; that's what we'll call him for the purpose of this example. Mike was only seventeen back in 2001, when it happened.

Still a senior in high school, he was driving his truck to school one morning when another vehicle flew over the median, and landed on top of him. Paramedics rushed him to the hospital, where his parents were informed he might lose his leg.

Mike's mother, who attends *Life Church* in Mission Viejo, California, asked the pastors for prayer that night, that her son would keep his leg and receive a full recovery. She made a specific and unapologetic request of God, and refused to grovel.

That following Sunday, we met up with her in the church lobby. At that moment, she was talking to the esteemed, co-founder of the *Four Square Church*, who by now was an aging widow. So, we stood around in a small circle as Mike's mother described her son's condition. And that's when the elderly widow said … "Well, don't forget, all things happen for a reason."

Mike's mother, a fiery redhead, almost blew her stack right there in the church lobby. "What?" she spat. "What's that supposed to mean? There's no reason for God to take my son's leg!"

All of us should be more like Mike's mom. Just because people say something over and over, does not make it 'truth.' Mike's mother knew the accident was not part of God's plan for her son, and hardly the reason she brought him into this world. It was, in fact, a PERVERSION of God's plan. Mike's mom wouldn't stand for the old-church muck, because she knew about this oldie, but goodie:

John 10:10
"The thief comes to steal, **kill and destroy,** but I have come to give them life more abundantly."

Realizing the car-crash was not sent by God, she immediately ran to Him for help, which is probably why her son was up and around **in less than a month!**

A few weeks after young Mike's accident, another child across town was struck by tragedy. We went to see Trinity Broadcast Network personality, Hal Lindsey, speak at *Mariners' Church*, in Irvine, California, regarding the 9/11 attacks. As we waited for Hal Lindsey to come out, we made the mistake of picking up the *Mariners'* church bulletin. Inside was an article about a toddler who had just been diagnosed with brain cancer. In the article, the father of the child was quoted as saying, "We know the Lord is doing this for a reason, so we have to stay strong."

It was yet another example of good and decent people being hoodwinked into believing that God predestinates hardcore evil for some purpose. No doubt they never prayed for help. Why should they? According to what they had been taught, the evil was sent by God. Following through on that logic, praying for help would defy God's will, right?

Sewing And Reaping

Now, had the cancer struck an obese, fifty-year old, chain-smoker with atrocious eating habits, we can see how the 'all things happen for a reason' thing might actually apply. Many times, the law of 'sowing and reaping' is the reason for our demise.

Church leaders repeatedly fail to clarify the difference. Was it the result of our own doing…another person's evil used against us…or the work of the unseen predator? Instead, of exploring the true cause, they soak every tragedy in the same God-marinade. How tawdry and lazy.

The Judeo-Christian God knows perfectly well, that if He wants to strike up a conversation with mankind, injecting us with a deadly disease, or burning down our house, is not the way to go about it; in the same way that terrorists bombing innocent civilians standing around a vegetable cart, is also not the way to win the affections of the townsfolk.

Let's not confuse man's fallen ways with God's. The New Testaments clearly reflects His consistent pattern of outreach toward mankind.

Matthew 7:11
If you being mortal, know how to give good things
to your children, how much more will your Father
in Heaven give good gifts to those who ask?

Jeremiah 29:11
For I know the thoughts that I think toward you,
says the Lord, thoughts of peace, and not of evil,
to give you a future and a hope.

Luke 2:14
Glory to God in the highest,
And peace on Earth;
Good will toward all men!

The Ultimate Outrage!

There once was a certain Christian man (a work colleague), at a certain computer-repair company, located on Ball Road, in Anaheim, California, and we got into a discussion one day about this very topic.

At the time, he was an avid proponent of the 'all things happen for a reason' teaching, and what he said in support of this was the most outrageous and ignorant thing that any of us had ever heard. The question was this:

"What if your son gets into a car crash and loses both of his legs? What would be the reason for that?"

At the time, his son was only eight years old, so the man's answer was shocking. He said:

> "Well, how do we know there's not a reason for God doing that, and we just don't see it at the time?"

Then, right on queue, he shrugged his shoulders and said, "The Lord gives and the Lord takes away."

Let's pause for a moment to recover. We need to vigorously protect ourselves against interpretations like this, because they are reckless and dangerous.

Like so many Christians, he quoted the Book of Job (discussed in an earlier chapter), about a man whose ten children were murdered, his house gutted, and was then struck with painful, oozing boils all over his body. In fact, the man's flesh was so mutilated, his own friends could not recognize him when they arrived. In the midst of his excruciating, mental and physical anguish, Job said, "The Lord gives and the Lord takes away."

> Question: Since when is it OK to take the advice of a man who is delirious with fever and pain?

And yet, this answer is given in Christian counseling sessions around the world. Their pastors failed to teach him who the true destroyer is. Do all things happen for a reason? Well, that depends on what it is. Only good and perfect things come from Heaven. Do not allow anyone to tell you any different.

Myth 7

Nothing Bad Can Happen

Unless God Allows It?

We hardly need Bible scripture to shoot this one down. Just turn on the six o'clock news and you'll see things happening all day long that God never allowed.

In the fall of 2005, Larry King hosted a panel of America's most popular Evangelical and Pentecostal ministers, to discuss 'the spiritual meaning' of Hurricane Katrina. During the show, King asked the ministers this choice question:

"Can God stop evil if He wants to?"

Straight down the line, each minister answered:

"Yes, He can…but He doesn't."

Although the ministers in question are good and decent men, their answer was reckless. They perpetuated the myth that 'nothing bad can happen unless God allows it.' Preachers who make this allegation fail to acknowledge three, distinct portals by which evil enters this world:

1. When **evil people** destroy us

2. When we **destroy ourselves** by our own devises

3. And when the **unseen predator** destroys us

In past chapters we amplified how Portals 1 and 2 involve mankind's own abuse of free will; events in which the Judeo-Christian God has no involvement. In fact, morgues all over the country are stacked high with victims of these two portals.

Portal 3, however, is something that very few people will ever accept; obviously because talk of an invisible predator sounds too fantastic. And yet, Christ and the Apostles identified him as the murderer of all mankind, again and again.

Also interesting to note is that they fingered him as the 'ruler of the air'…in other words, the ruler of our weather system. The Apostle Paul describes his powers in Ephesians 2:2 and 6:12, as:

1. The [dark] prince and power of the air…

2. Principalities and dark powers in the heavenlies.

'Heavenlies' was the ancient way of saying 'atmosphere.' Again, what you believe about devils and demons is your own business, but according to Christ and the Apostles, these 'powers in the air' have the ability to whip our weather system into violent, cyclonic events…at will.

The most recent and highly suspicious example of this occurred in the New Orleans French Quarter. This is the district where 'true sinners' gather to drink, smoke, gamble and fornicate; and yet, the entire red-light district came away **totally unscathed by flood waters,** while the weak, sick and ignorant were drowned wholesale. The event had all the markings of the unseen predator.

Chips 'n Dip

Because of their sloppy answer, the preachers in question presented the Judeo-Christian God as snacking on chips 'n dip with His feet up on the coffee table, as humanity gets stuffed through the sausage grinder. Just once, they should man up and explained how things really work.

> The truth is, many times evil is so strong…and crafty…by the time we call out for God's help, it's already too late!

For this reason, should we come under the supernatural, protective power of Christ NOW, during times of peace, BEFORE another disaster strikes?

Most people don't acknowledge His existence until a crisis hits, and by then, it's too late. They have already been ravaged.

And why should they turn to God? They have been taught all their lives that it's God who dispatched the crisis in the first place. With no way out, their entrapment is now complete; hence, the reason for this book.

Nothing bad can happen unless God allows it? Should we really lay down for this notion?

Billy Graham seems to think so.

Inquiring Minds Want to Know

Another painful example of glossing over the issues is the Reverend Billy Graham. In September, 2001, Reverend Graham was invited by George W. Bush to speak at Washington's National Cathedral, to shed light on the 9/11 terror attacks.

The whole country sucked in its collective breath, expecting Reverend Graham to offer an explanation. Hysterically, he delivered only predictable rhetoric:

> "How do we understand something like this? Why does God allow evil like this to take place? I have been asked **hundreds of times** why God allows tragedy and suffering."

Here is proof from America's most beloved preacher that the whole world is asking this question, and has been asking for thousands of years. As such, one would assume that he might have researched the matter by now, but it seems he never did.

> "I have to confess that I really do not know the answer totally, even to my own satisfaction."

Reverend Graham is a good man, but how is it that after sixty years in ministry he never discovered the answers, flashing like neon signs in front of him? Predictably he concluded with this:

> "I have to accept, by faith, that God is sovereign, and that He is a God of love and mercy…"

Why did the Reverend Graham omit the truth about why evil things happen? Like so many, he tried to suggest that God could have stopped 9/11, when it is all too obvious that He cannot interfere with free will.

Although Reverend Graham did not say it on this particular day, the above discourse is invariably followed by…"He does it because He loves us,"…but was every wit implied.

The State of California

Had the preachers in question done their homework (which is what they get paid to do), they would have remembered that the Judeo-Christian God already stated in the Ten Commandments what He does, **and does not allow.**

Hence, any deviation from those Commandments, to a greater or lesser degree, is not something He would allow. Let's put this into practical terms:

> California's speed limit is 65 mph. Then a drunk driver speeds down the freeway at 100 mph, and kills someone.

> Question: Who allowed this to happen?
>   Was it the State of California?

No, the State already stipulated what it does not allow. Notice also that California's laws can be broken at any moment, but that does not mean the State allows it. Here is another example:

> You've told your teenager never to use drugs, but she dabbles in crystal-meth, and nearly dies.

> Question: Who allowed this to happen?
>   Was it the parent?

No, the parent already said what he does not allow, but the child paid no attention. Had the preachers done their homework, they would have remembered that man has been doing things that God does not allow, as far back as **Genesis Chapter 3**, when he first defected from God. This now brings us to a point that many Christians and Catholics cannot accept:

God is **NOT** sovereign over everything!

On the contrary, our decisions are just as sovereign as God's. The meaning of this next statement is so in-your-face, it's a wonder why it has eluded church leaders for so long (or maybe they just don't want to see it).

> Exodus 13:17
> God did not lead them through Philistine country, even though that was the shorter route, for God said, "War is raging in that land, and if the people see it, they might become frightened, **CHANGE THEIR MINDS,** and go back to Egypt."

Notice, that God **ADMITS** the Israelites had the power to **CHANGE THEIR MINDS**, which is exactly what they did. Three million people said, "No thanks, we don't want to enter the Promised Land," and chose instead to live in tents for forty years. Notice that God was NOT sovereign over their decision. In the end He said, "OK, this generation never will see the Promised Land."

We now have a snapshot as to how powerful free will can be; to the extent that we can cancel out God's will and implement our own. This is, of course, not a good idea, but the point is, it can be done.

Worth Their Wages?

In response to Billy Graham's claim that God is sovereign over all things, the Exodus event proves otherwise, as does man's early defection in Genesis Chapter 3. And now this, from the New Testament:

> Matthew 13:58
>
> And He did not do many miracles in Nazareth, because **they did not believe** in Him [so He left}.

> Matthew 23:37
>
> "Jerusalem, Jerusalem…how often I wanted to protect you like baby chicks…but you **would not let Me.**"

In both events, God had no choice but to **LEAVE** because the people would not go along with Him. Perhaps we are now in a better position to answer Larry King's questions.

If preachers cannot effectively answer questions that strike at the heart of man, perhaps they are not worth their wages.

Can God stop evil if He wants to? Is it true that nothing bad can happen unless God allows it? The problem with these questions is that there are far too many reasons why He cannot, the main one of which is…many of us don't acknowledge God, until it's already too late.

What about the rest of the time?

Myth 8

Testing.

Does God Really Test Us?

Here's a quick word of advice…church people are very fond of their suffering…so this is probably not something you should talk about at Church Bingo.

Whereas the other fabrications highlighted in this book suggest man's own complicity, this one is by far the deadliest, because it makes an extremely bold-faced insinuation:

God hurts people…just to see how they'll act.

To perpetuate the myth, the church swiftly cites the Old Testament Book of Job. As discussed in an earlier chapter, he was the righteous, wealthy, and somewhat nervous man who lived during ancient times, in the region of today's Iraq.

In the account, Job's ten children were murdered by barbarian hordes, his property demolished, and livestock carried away. About an hour later, he was struck head-to-toe with excruciating boils. For relief, he lanced them open with shards of broken pottery.

The once-happy man was now reduced to a bleeding flesh-pile in the corner of his burned-out house; and all in the span of a day. The church, of course, claims that God brought on the whole thing.

For centuries, church leaders have been unable to reconcile the sordid mess of Job. To compensate for their abysmal ignorance, endless fabrications have emerged that are not only irrational...but also **perverse.**

Trial By Ordeal

First, Job is identified at the start of the scroll as "perfect and upright." Hence, it is incorrect to assume that he did something bad to deserve his destruction. In fact, his profile matches that of many people today who are struck by tragedy and never did a thing to deserve it.

Another conjecture is that Job was set aside for destruction. And yet, according to basic Christian doctrine, no one was ever 'set aside' for destruction...except Christ.

Nevertheless, the church insists that his destruction "was all part of God's plan." When asked why it happened, the stock answer is, "To bless him at the end of the ordeal."

It's a vulgar summation that smacks awfully of the Catholic Church's medieval form of torture, known as 'Trial by Ordeal.' In this ritual, poor souls were tied up and drowned at the bottom of a river. If they rose to the top, they were guilty. If they stayed under, they were innocent. Either way, they lost their lives.

If we take a closer look at just a few verses in Chapter 1, it becomes apparent that none of the above conjectures are true. What really happened is that Job took a **GAMBLE**…and he lost. It all started with this verse:

Job 1:5
Job sent for his [grown] sons and blessed them; and rising up early every morning, he made burnt offerings for each of them, because Job said, "**It may be** my sons have sinned and cursed God in their hearts." Job did this continually.

Here, Job had a suspicion that his sons were up to no good. Whether his suspicions were real or imagined, inexplicably, he never took action. Many parents ignore red flag areas today (such as kids hiding weapons in their closets), and the results are disastrous. Even so, there is no indication that his sons were involved in contraband. The figments were purely of his imagination.

Whatever the case, Job was the richest man in town and had unlimited resources at his disposal. He could have sent servants to spy on his sons; he could have cut off their allowance, but he did nothing to ease his suspicions. Job was like the police officer who failed to call in for back-up. Christians will now argue, "Wait a minute, Job prayed for them and sacrificed every day!"

No, that is incorrect. Chopping, burning, and chanting **do not qualify as prayer.** To drive the point all the way home, when was the last time you prayed like this?

- It may be my kids will get shot at school
- It may be my house will burn down
- It may be I'll get hit by a bus
- It may be I'll get cancer

It doesn't take rocket science to see that Job's obsessive-compulsive behavior hardly qualifies as prayer, in the same way that chanting over rosary beads ever will. In all of Chapter 1, he never once looked up the sky and ASKED for help. In terms of the Judeo-Christian God:

He had not…because he asked not.

Like so many of us, Job was the snapshot of a man who took a gamble. He attempted to do things on his own…and lost.

Our Daily Bread?

But let's not beat up on Job. After all, he lived in heathen territory, and had no one to teach him how to pray correctly; which brings us to the next point. This general lack of knowledge concerning prayer shows up everywhere in today's pop culture.

Take for instance, paranormal investigators. We see them on television trying to 'cleanse' a house of evil entities, and for protection they pray the Lord's Prayer. Walking from room to room they chant, "Our Father, who art in heaven, give us our daily bread." But the question is:

What does 'daily bread'

Have to do with fighting evil spirits?

Wouldn't it be more logical to ask for **protection**? But this is not their fault. Like Job, the world at large has never been taught to pray correctly. Many times the entities return to that house, knowing they are not obligated to obey humans who don't know how to execute authority over them. Other times the spirits leave right away, knowing their job is done. (They made 'believers' out of yet another thousand people watching from home. Unbeknownst to us, they do compete for our souls.)

Suddenly, another reason emerges for Job's destruction. It was the deadly cocktail of ignorance and complacency, and God had nothing to do with either. Who knows how long Job's useless sacrificing and chanting went on?

Eventually, God threw up His hands and, speaking to the devil, He said, "Behold, all that he has is in your hands."

How long has God been trying to reach us? He will only wait for so long. If we don't come around eventually, there is nothing more He can do. By the time the disaster hits, it's already too late.

Job got no protection because He never asked for any!

By teaching falsehoods about Job to the public at large, the church implicates the Judeo-Christian God in a ten-count murder rap, massive property damage, assault with a deadly weapon, looting, and egregious bodily injury. And from this pot of bubbling, boiling dribble stems the deadliest doctrine of all.

TESTING!

Don't Ask, Don't Tell

Most Christians and Catholics don't ask the hard questions about God to clear up the quagmire. Christians don't ask because they are asleep, and Catholics don't because…well…they're not allowed to.

When preachers talk about 'testing', they usually mean everything from sickness, disease, bankruptcy, infidelity, property damage, loss of jobs and income, and heartbreak of every kind. They'll say things like:

- Yes, God will test you; He tested Jesus in the wilderness, He'll test you too
- Testing perfects us
- Trials and tribulations make us stronger
- If we don't have trials, how will we ever see God's power to rescue us?
- And everyone's personal favorite…He does it because He loves us!

This teaching has caused mankind intense psychological strain over the centuries because it demands that we cherish our suffering, and pay it homage, as though it were a holy thing. In other words…smile for the camera…as your whole life crumbles around you. The result is, a breach between us and God that is many times irreparable…but it's a breach based on scripture that does not exist.

Suffering ... Live On TV

Christian television is littered with talk-show hosts boasting about their trials and ordeals. Invariably, they equate their experiences with that of Job's, claiming they were elected by God to suffer for Him.

In 2002, the popular minister, Juanita Bynum, appeared on Trinity Broadcast Network. On this particular night, she interviewed a certain young woman whose first husband was killed within a year after their wedding, and her second husband died just as quickly. Of the events, the twice-bereaved widow said:

> "God took my first husband and broke me, and just when I couldn't grieve any more, He took the second one, and broke me again! And He did all that to prepare me for ministry!"

Then, the woman started wailing, whereupon Juanita Bynum jumped up and indicted her into the office of 'prophetess' for all her suffering.

Around the same time, Pastor Marilyn Hickey interviewed a guest on her TBN program. It was a woman who had been beaten, sodomized and left for dead in an alley. Of the rape, the victim said:

> "God **wanted** this to happen to me! He **needed** this to happen to me, so that I would know how to minister to other victims!"

Pastor Hickey nodded dutifully, as though her guest had spoken some sort of Gospel truth. One could tell that the women meant well and were only trying to help others, but their conclusion about God's involvement in the crimes was woefully misguided.

To persons untrained in scripture, this type of gibberish might actually ring true. In fact, it sounds sweetly sanctimonious; but had the women read the scriptures correctly, they would have discovered that God is **powerful enough** to set them up in ministry, without factoring rape and death into the equation. In fact, notice that Abraham, the very Father of the Judeo-Christian faith, was called **quietly and graciously**, and never fell victim to such crimes.

The very idea that TBN allowed this to be aired is outrageous. What if an incest survivor were watching on those nights? The information they were being fed was, "God wanted this to happen to you."

Ministers who make such reckless claims should be summoned to court, sued for mental and emotional abuse, and lose their non-profit licensing. A few months later, John Hagee, a highly respected pastor in San Antonio, shouted this into the camera:

> "If you love something and care about it with all your heart, you can forget about holding on to it. Rest assured that God will test you and **rip it away** from you!"

Hopefully, no parents of missing children were watching that day. Later that year, America's favorite people's preacher, Bishop T. D. Jakes, told a crowd of millions watching from home:

> "If God has elected you to be tested...consider yourself *blessed!*"

Simply put, the 'testing' doctrine is the cherished, church darling that may never ever be quashed until the end of time.

Testing, Testing … One, Two, Three

Now, whereas the dangerous commentary highlighted in this chapter are widely accepted as true, the good news is, they can easily be shot down with just a small handful of scriptures; but it cannot be done with the English translation. The following excerpts come from the original Greek texts, which disprove the doctrine, straight down the line. Take a look:

James 1:13

If any man is tested, let him not say 'I am tested of God' for God cannot be tested by evil, nor does He test anyone.

James 1:14

And where do tests come from, but your own covetousness (not from heaven).

Matthew 6:13

Lead us not into testing, but deliver us from evil.

Matthew 26:41

Watch and pray so that you do not enter testing.

1st Corinthians 10:13

With every test, God makes an escape...

Notice the last verse which states God makes an escape out of every test. Following through on this logic, what fruit would there be in the test, if it's cut short?

Those of you who own a Bible will notice right away that the English translation uses the word 'temptation' (and its derivatives) in the afore-mentioned verses, but the word 'temptation' was never used in the original Greek texts.

The New Testament was **ALTERED** to make it appear that God tests us with heartbreak and tragedy, when in fact, Christ and the Apostles said He does not.

Theologians are invited to look up Strong's Concordance, Greek Word Nos. 3985 and 3986. Theologians will try to reject these findings as taken out of context. If so, they must also reject Strong's Exhaustive Concordance, Thayer's Greek-English Lexicon, Sovereign Grace's Hebrew-Greek-English Interlinear Bible, and the original Greek texts, because all bodies of work cry the same data.

Theologians should also take notice that the Apostle James said we are **not allowed** to tell people that God tests us. His instruction merits another look.

James 1:13

"If any man is tested, **let him not say** 'I am tested of God'…"

No doubt, the verses in question were stealthily altered after the death of the Apostles, to suit rogue elements inside the early church, in their attempt to frighten the world. Now, let's examine the glaring contradictions side-by-side:

The church teaches: God leads us into testing.

But Christ leads us **away** from it! Matthew 6:13

The church teaches: God sends the testing.

But James said tests **do not** come from God. James 1:14

The church teaches: We should honor testing.

But Christ warned us to **stay out** of them!   Matthew 26:41

The church teaches: Testing perfects us.

But Paul said God makes an **escape** from them!

1ˢᵗ Corinthians 10:13

OK, so whom should we believe? The church, or the original texts written by the Apostles?

You be the judge.

Intellectual Property Violations

Although the translation effort of the Old and New Testaments is generally a splendid accomplishment, the damage they have caused over the centuries is virtually irreversible.

Bible corporations should be required to explain why the altered verses have been allowed to stand all this time, but it's all too clear how they can get away with it. None of the original authors are alive to challenge them.

The Old Testament, however, is still the intellectual property of the Sovereign State of Israel. Why should the Anglo translations be allowed to override the original writings? Perhaps because the Israeli government never challenged the Bible companies either. Meantime, whole sermons have been concocted, and Sunday school lessons peppered, with analogies based on scriptures that **do not exist**. Take for instance this English bastardization:

Job 1:8
"Have you **considered** My servant job…?"

In this scenario, God allegedly abandoned Job and turned him over to Satan for wholesale slaughter; but God never said anything of the sort. Here is the original Hebrew:

> Said the Lord unto Satan, "**Appoint care** for My servant Job, for there is none like him in all the Earth…"

The phrase **'appoint care'** is listed in Strong's Exhaustive Concordance as Hebrew Word Nos. 7760 and 3820, which means: **'to place caution.'** In other words, God warned Satan to **stay away** from the man. The 1898 Robert Young Literal Translation presents a more accurate picture:

> Have you **set your heart against** My servant Job, because there is none like him…?

Clearly, Satan started to obsess over the man, and God told him to back off. Alas, only the false interpretation became canonized as the official church doctrine, but is completely disqualified by the original Hebrew. Technically, the Old Testament can be construed as a signed Affidavit because it is the intellectual property of the Jews. As such, since when is it acceptable to alter a court document?

OK, So What's Still On The Table?

Now, it is true that several statements in the New Testament warn that testing cannot be avoided. Take a look:

James 1:2-3
Count it as joy...because the testing of your faith produces endurance.

Philippians 1:29
It has been granted to you to suffer with Christ.

By all appearance, these statements might actually confirm what preachers have been alleging all along. However, they fail to acknowledge that God said He would NOT send the tests, and that He would rescue us from ALL of them.

Sickness, disease, poverty and misery are NOT part of any package that comes out of Heaven. The Judeo-Christian God does not 'have a disease' that He can give you, nor does He own a 'poor house' that He can put you in. The Apostle Paul explained it this way:

Galatians 3:13-14

For He was made the curse, so that we could be **rescued** from the curse; and so that Gentiles could receive the Blessing of Abraham.

The blessings and cursing are detailed in Deuteronomy Chapter 28 of the Old Testament. Once you read the curses, in Verses 15-68, you will understand what Christ rescued us from, which is: sickness, disease, poverty and misery.

The blessings are outlined in the same chapter, Verses 1-14. Once you read those, you will understand what great gifts you have received, which are: health, prosperity, success and happiness. The question is, have we all accepted these blessings?

So if disease, poverty and misery were taken off the table two thousand years ago, what did Paul mean when he said, "You were called to suffer for Christ"?

He was talking about the 'normal' motions of life.

LIFE! … It Can Be A Real Drag!

We all agree that even the 'normal' motions of life have a way of testing us to the limit, right? We get tested at the age of three to see if we qualify for that uptown preschool; then we get tested all the way through high school graduation. Before too long, we get tested for a driver's licenses, then college finals, and sometimes the doctor calls us back for more tests. Then we get tested by colleagues at work, and after that, rush-hour traffic.

The mortgage company tests us every month, and, oh yes, don't forget your belligerent boss, long lines at the grocery store, meddling in-laws, and bills piled high on the kitchen table. Next come neighbors who run the lawn-mower at six in the morning (on a Saturday), and loud-mouthed teenagers who think they know it all.

The normal motions of life, however, DO NOT include bloodshed, heartbreak, violent crimes, poverty and disease! God is not ignorant in the matter of our limits. He knows we can take only so much. And that is why it makes no sense for Him to pile on more tests, on top of those already presented by life. For this reason, He offers His hand as our Personal Life Coach. Take a look:

Matthew 11:28-30

Come to Me, all of you who are over-worked and stressed-out, and I will give you plenty of rest. My requirements are very light, and I am very gentle and humble. In Me, you will find rest for your tired soul.

The Upper and the Downer

Even now, many people will not be able to grasp the notion that God wants them to live in peace. This could be because they are 'test junkies.' They need the crescendo and decrescendo, the upper and the downer. They thrive on chaos.

Like Job, they nurse unrequited compulsions to believe that there must be something wrong, when in fact, everything is right.

The world is filled with people just like that, and so are churches. Many begin their new life in Christ and never lived so well, but soon they become bored with their newfound serenity. Next thing you know, they'll go to their pastor for counseling.

"Pastor Bob, I'm really bored. What should I do?"

Systematically, Pastor Bob tells them, "Well, it's time to ask God for some tests. If you want to spice things up, ask God for tests, trials and tribulation."

This is probably the most dangerous instruction a minister could ever give to anyone. God already stated **He does not test anyone.** Therefore, it stands to reason that whatever shows up at their door…

DID NOT COME FROM GOD!

As a result, those who have listened to this ghoulish advice, suffered many losses; everything from jobs, homes, businesses, marriages, even life and limb…because they gave it **permission to enter.**

Once the tragedy hits, Pastor Bob is at a total loss and cannot explain the events. To compensate for this, he immediately coddles the idea of human suffering.

"Well, count it all joy," he says. "Don't forget, it's a blessing to suffer for Christ."

The Real Agenda

The truth is, testing is not necessary for our spiritual growth. Its sole agenda is to break our hearts and make us cry. It gets us to hate God, shout obscenities, and never trust Him again.

And behind each heartbreaking event is the unseen predator, who goes deeper into hiding (and the church helps him to do so), while the Judeo-Christian God takes all the blame.

Instead of counseling these complainers to ask for testing, ministers should point them toward healthier, more useful preoccupations, such as: volunteering at a homeless shelter, signing up for foster-care, working weekends at a youth facility, continuing their education, political activities, charity fund-raisers, or starting a home-business. And what about putting together care packages for troops or prisoners?

After all, serving others is a far more noble preoccupation than the suckling of one's own restless flesh.

From now on, whenever you hear sermons that glorify human suffering, listen defensively…as though to protect your life!

Pastor Tony Soprano

That's what we'll call him, just between us. Back in the year 2001, a colorful preacher came to our Orange County church. He had a thick, New York-gangster accent, wore a double-breasted suit, and had a slick, Al Capone look about him. The only thing missing were 'spats.' We got a big kick out of him. For many months after his visit, we affectionately referred to him as 'Pastor

Soprano.' Who knows, he probably was a real, ex-crime boss who at one time or another collided with Christ and lived to tell about it. 'Pastor Soprano' said the most profound thing that any of us had ever heard:

De Fada' loves youz guyz
So don' get so good at sufferink down heah'
Coz when youz get ta heaven
Youz ain't gonna' need sufferink
Sufferink don't change nuttn'
God loves us de same way
For betta' or woys'
And He loves us de same way
Wheda we're rich or poor
Healt'y or sick … happy or sad
So, if our sufferink doesn't change a 'ting
Youz might as well be rich, happy, and healt'y!

Hey, let's all go to that church!

Myth 9

Vows of Poverty.

Does God Really

Demand Them?

Does the Judeo-Christian God require 'vows of poverty' from humans? Does being poor really bring us closer to God?

Well, that depends on what God you're referring to. If it's the Judeo-Christian God, the answer is no...***never!***

This is actually the church's very own Ponzi scheme, and has not only infected Christendom, but many Eastern religions as well. In some religions, poverty is considered to be the gateway to 'holiness' but not all of us are so easily hoodwinked.

EVERYBODY KNOWS IT'S THE

GATEWAY TO CRIME!

As a result of this doctrine many generations have been plunged into the headlock cycle of misery, from which very few ever recover.

Poverty's byproducts are: starvation, humiliation, illiteracy, drug addiction, never-ending need and hunger, lack of medical treatment, shattered self-esteem, human trafficking, hopelessness, violent crimes, and untold human suffering.

Anecdotes have to work across the board. We cannot throw something against the wall just to see what sticks. For instance, are you prepared to tell a Somali youngster with a bloated belly and flies crawling into his mouth, that poverty is 'holy'? What about those youngsters in the ghetto across town from you?

Money … The Answer To Everything?

Whenever church leaders, especially in the Catholic sector, glorify poverty as something to be desired, they seem to forget about this little problem:

> Ecclesiastes 10:19(c) & 7:12
> Money answers everything…Wisdom is protection,
> just as money is protection.

As they say in New York … badda-bing-badda-boong!

This was written by Israel's King Solomon, considered by all theologians to be the 'wisest man that ever lived.' Therefore, if the world's smartest guy said money is a good thing, why should anyone practice poverty? And what about this naughty one?

Proverbs 10:22
The blessing of the Lord makes us rich, and He adds no sorrow with it.

What a glaring difference between the original message concerning money, and the tawdry, mainstream teaching. As far back as Old Testament times, money was well-regarded and celebrated.

Psalm 35:27(b)
The Lord has pleasure in the prosperity of His servants.

There is not much that pious critics of money can say to argue these declarations. Centuries later, the Apostle Paul said God wants us to have money, enough for ourselves, and some left over to give away to others. Take a look:

2nd Corinthians 9:8
God is able to turn all favor toward you, so that you will have sufficiency in all things and for every good work.

Love and Lust

The poverty doctrine originated with this often misquoted statement from the New Testament:

1st Timothy 6:10
"The **love** of money is the root of all evil..."

We often hear this quoted as: "Money is the root of all evil." But that is incorrect. The Apostle said...**the lust for it...the greed for it**...is the root of all evil. He never said money is evil.

It is not money that commits murder and embezzlement, but man's greed for it; in the same way that aspirin does not kill people, but ingesting the whole bottle will. Additionally, ignorant money management can also bring destruction, but how is that money's fault? Take a look:

1st Timothy 6:10
For **the love of money** is a root of all evil. Some people, eager for money, have wandered from the faith and **pierced themselves** with many tribulations.

Mainstream church leaders fail to acknowledge that people throughout the world enjoy great wealth, in the Christian and non-Christian sectors, many of whom are not corrupt, but well-balanced, happy people; not to mention, their children are well cared for.

Critics will now point to the corrupt CEOs of Wall Street, but everyone knows they were hardly 'well-balanced' to begin with.

Child Support Payments

Taking vows of poverty began with the early Catholic Church, around the same time that celibacy was enforced upon its priests, circa 1000 AD.

It is said that priests were forced to take celibacy vows during this time, not for spiritual development, but because they fathered too many children out of wedlock, and the Vatican could no longer keep up with the subsequent child support claims. Hence, priests were forced to vow poverty and celibacy.

Vows of poverty were also forced upon commoners, who had very little to begin with. This presented a stark contrast between the Vatican's decadent opulence, and the hungry commoner's dismal existence. In answer to this complaint, the Vatican's argument has not changed in centuries:

"Why do you question what God has asked of you?"

The problem is, God never did ask for it. Contrary to the fables, New Testament records show this practice was **never** a commandment, in the same way that flagellation (the beating and cutting of oneself) ever was. Nevertheless, the doctrine wormed its way into the mainstream Christian sector just as quickly, and became its **shameful** way of life, until the mid-1940s, when it was finally challenged by several Pentecostal preachers.

The Great Commission ... It Costs Money!

Unlike the Old Testament patriarchs, today's followers of Christ are given a whole new job description, called 'the Great Commission' which is to spread the Gospel all over the world.

But this new commission costs a lot of money. In fact, the expenses involved are staggering! No one is going to argue that running an organization encompassing the entire globe costs money. Satellite time, utilities, salaries, equipment, transportation, and general operating expenses are absolutely crushing!

However, some questions still linger.

Several mega preachers recently came under fire for their opulent lifestyles, and were the subject of a Congressional hearing, spear-headed by Iowa State Senator, Chuck Grassley. Some of the ministers in question refused to cooperate; but why? Doesn't that make them look more suspect? By taking 'the fifth' what are they trying to hide? (That's not an accusation; it's just a question.)

For instance, how do three ocean-front mansions valued at $5 million each, owned by a certain network and purchased with viewer donations, serve the spreading of the Gospel?

And why should televangelists be allowed to call for donations…"to spread the Gospel around the world"…when portions of the money are being spent to purchase ocean-front property?

Wouldn't it be more truthful to say…"We are collecting donations to buy ocean-front property"?

Of course, they cannot say that because no one would donate ever again. When questioned about these excessive spending habits, the stock answer is, "Well, Abraham was a millionaire in his time, therefore, we also have the right to live like that."

Yes but, Abraham was not handed the Great Commission. His only 'commission' was to find grass for his goats, and produce an heir.

More Wasteful Spending

Not everything qualifies as a 'Call For Donations.' Take for instance one preacher who, back in 2005, boasted about all the expensive gifts he brings home to his wife. He took her hand, held it up to the camera and showed everyone the five carat diamond ring he had just purchased for her.

"I've bought my wife ten of these, and she says she doesn't want any more, but I can't help it. I just love to buy her gifts!"

Twenty minutes later, he asked for donations for his church's building fund. Well, if he has money to purchase ten diamonds valued at mega-thousands each, wouldn't it have made more sense to buy her *three* rings (let's be fair), and contribute the rest toward his own building fund? After all, his wife said she didn't want any more!

The stock defense to this would be, "Well, that's what they said to the woman with the alabaster jar."

In that particular incident, Jesus attended a dinner party at a nobleman's house. Then a woman came in, broke open a very expensive jar of perfume, and poured it over His feet. Several of the guests muttered, "What is she doing that for? She could have sold that perfume and given the money to the poor." But Jesus rebuked them and said, "Leave her alone. She is doing this to prepare Me for burial." The woman's good deed, however, cannot be used to justify frivolous spending, because Christ was **scheduled for crucifixion,** whereas the televangelists are not. They have to raise money for world outreach, remember?

Another question is, while they are spending these exorbitant amounts, is there anyone in their church assembly that needs help?

1st John 3:17

> But whoever has this world's goods, and sees his
> brother in need, and shuts up his heart from him,
> how does the love of God abide in him?

Around the same time, a popular Bishop's wife appeared on Christian television and whispered into the camera, "Shhhh, it's a secret. Don't tell Bishop. We're taking up an offering for his birthday." Not all requests for donations qualify as 'spreading the Gospel.'

Payin' It Forward

Wealth, in the healthy, well-balanced sense, is a widely celebrated state of being throughout the Testaments. In fact, money satisfies our mortgage payments, puts our kids through school, pays medical bills, allows us to visit great holiday spots, dresses us in fine clothing, pays off our vehicles, fixes holes in our roofs, and hopefully leaves behind a little something for the kids.

Therefore, the question is not whether mega preachers should be allowed to have money, but how well they pay if forward to the people.

Take for instance, Pastor Creflo Dollar, of College Park, Georgia. He has a program in place wherein his church helps single mothers to pay their bills. Now, that's a valuable service that no one can shake a stick at.

Was Christ Really Poor?

Christians and Catholics insist, with teeth-clenching, white-knuckle conviction, that Christ was poor; therefore, we should also be. It's a misconception that began with this event:

> Luke 2:7
> And she brought forth her firstborn Son, wrapped Him in **swaddling cloths**, and laid Him in a manger, because there was **no room** at the inn.

This account speaks of Joseph and Miriam, the night that Christ was born. (That's her real name, by the way; there is no one named 'Mary' in the original text.)

First, swaddling cloths are not 'rags.' The word 'swaddle' means to 'blanket' and is a wrapping technique still used today on newborns by hospitals worldwide.

Second, just because Joseph and Miriam couldn't get a room

at the inn, does not mean they could not pay for it. It simply means there was 'no vacancy'!

In the weeks before Jesus was born, historical records show that Cesar Augustus called for a worldwide census to be taken, around 8 BC. This meant citizens throughout the Roman Empire were forced to drop whatever they were doing, and scramble back to their hometowns to register with the Roman government.

And this event is what caused the massive over-crowding in Bethlehem recorded in Luke, Chapter 2. Miriam gave birth inside an animal stable because:

"There was no room at the inn!"

There is a big difference between 'no money' and 'no vacancy.' Furthermore, Joseph was a carpenter. Today's equivalent of that profession is the 'General Contractor.' It was a vocation in real demand because there were no machines in that day.

The truth is, Christ was a **MILLIONAIRE** from the moment He was born. Take a look:

Matthew 2:11
When the three Mesopotamians had come into the house...they fell down and worshiped the babe...and opened their **treasures** to Him of **gold, frankincense, and myrrh.**

Few people understand the impact of this moment. Three astrologers from Mesopotamia had come a thousand miles to bring the infant 'gold bullion'…and other extremely expensive gifts. Notice also, they gave Him of their "treasures"…not sloppy seconds.

This deposit of treasure vaulted the young parents of Jesus into overnight wealth. Gold in those days was possessed only by royals, and if managed wisely, could easily sustain one throughout their lifetime.

Now, just as an interesting observation, why should heathen astrologers from far away Mesopotamia expect a Savior to be born? Why should they look for a bright star at all? Who was the Christ to them? They were, after all, heathen diviners of the Zodiac. Well, it just so happens, that one heathen nation in particular was actually looking for 'The Star.'

When Israel was released from Egypt fourteen hundred years before the birth of Christ, a heathen prophet named Balaam delivered a prophecy about 'The Star' coming out of Israel.

Balaam was a witch-doctor who was hired by an evil king to curse Israel with disease and destruction; but Balaam took one look at the three million people in the valley below, and instead of cursing them, began to prophesy. Take a look:

Numbers 24:17
I shall see Him, but not now; I shall behold Him, but not now. There will come a **Star** out of Jacob, and a [king] shall rise out of Israel...

Balaam lived in Pethor, located in Mesopotamia. It is a well-known, archeological fact that the Mesopotamians were fervent astrologers in that day. In fact, they built countless pyramids, called Ziggurats, to pacify their appetite for astrology, some dating back to 2,100 B.C.

No doubt, Balaam told the Mesopotamians to watch for 'The Star' and this information was passed down through the generations. It's a perfectly plausible scenario, otherwise how did the astrologers know 'The Star' was a Person and not just another star?

The point of this theory is it shows us a God who understands that money is a necessary component of life, and is willing to go out of His way to get it to us. The question is: have we opened the door to Him?

We joined a Catholic, online chat-group at www.catholic.com and pointed out to forum participants the priceless value of the gifts that were given to Jesus. We did this to see how they would react to the revelation that Christ was never poor.

One replied, "You're going to burn in hell!" (We still have the email.)

Another replied, "Mary never kept that money. She gave it away to the poor." (Actually, her name was Miriam; she was Jewish!)

Unfortunately, this is not recorded anywhere in the New Testament. As the most "blessed among women" such a charitable act would have been well recorded, as were all other words and deeds of Miriam. There is no doubt that the parents of Jesus lived modestly while Jesus was growing up. In fact, they set up house and home in Nazareth by the Sea of Galilee, a region known for its lack-luster environment. In fact, Nazareth has been called 'a slum.' And yet, it was the perfect place to hide one's gold…and child of destiny.

Seafront Property

The church insists that Jesus was 'homeless' based on this:

> Matthew 8:20
> Jesus said, "Foxes have holes and birds have nests, but I have nowhere to lay My head."

Now, just because Jesus' preaching schedule involved constant travel from place to place for almost four years, does not mean He was homeless. On the contrary, it simply meant He didn't stay in one place for too long. During His adult life, Jesus lived in the bustling, seafront city of Capernaum. Take a look:

> Matthew 4:13
> And leaving Nazareth, He came and dwelled in Capernaum, which is by the sea…

Archeology proves that Capernaum was a prime chunk of real estate in first century Judea. As the ancient hub of activity, Capernaum was well connected to every region throughout the Middle East, and experienced a constant stream of merchant trade year round. Capernaum was also prominently situated on the famous, intercontinental highway, known as 'Via Maris' running from Egypt and northward along the Mediterranean coast, through Capernaum, up to the Sea of Galilee, turning due east as far as Mesopotamia (probably the same roadway the astrologers took).

The population of Capernaum was highly varied with traveling merchants going to and from Roman outposts, and because of this constant saturation of travelers, Capernaum supplied a never-ending stream of customers for Jesus' carpentry business.

Jesus Christ, CEO

Jesus of Nazareth was not Gandhi. He was a Jew, and as such, viewed money as a necessary component of life, and so should we all. Therefore, alleging He was poor is like saying Jesus was a slacker, a loser, and a deadbeat who couldn't pay His bills. If we are to accept that He was the King of Kings and Lord of Lords, then without question, He was also the King of Finance…the King of Carpentry…and the King of Paying Bills on Time.

The Bloomingdale Robe

Evidence of His wealth followed Him all the way to the crucifixion. After the Roman soldiers drove stakes into Him, they actually 'gambled' for His robe. His robe was 'seamless' which, apparently, was the equivalent of a winter coat purchased from Bloomingdale's. Take a look:

John 19:23-24:

When the soldiers crucified Jesus, they took His garments **and made four parts**…for the tunic was without seam, woven from the top in one piece, and they said, "Let's not tear it apart, let's gamble for it."

Even after it was cut into four parts, it was still of great value. One Christmas season, we went to Bloomingdale's at Orange County's Fashion Island, located on Pacific Coast Highway. We were looking for a Christmas gift for a friend, a wallet perhaps, and couldn't find one for less than $400. In terms of value, our shopping trip to Bloomingdale's put the robe of Jesus into proper perspective.

By now the implications should be perfectly clear. Since poverty attacks every area of our lives, from food and clothing, to health and education, and every person's right to a sound future, the 'poverty message' falls flat on its face.

Poverty is not the gateway to 'holiness'. It's the gateway to crime and suffering.

April 13, 2029

At the end of the day, whatever your belief system may be, we cannot dismiss the fact that we have entered into some sort of new era; perhaps the Age of Disaster.

With the recent global, financial meltdown, world banks are secretly devising the one-world money system as we speak, described in the Book of Revelations. One third of the world is already under this new regime, in the form of the Euro.

On the other hand, it might already be here completely. Today we can exchange the Euro into the Yen, then into the Deutsche Mark, and back to the Euro, in about a minute.

Disasters we saw recently won't be the last. Apparently, they are just the hor'deurves of things to come. Many people reject this notion and say, "No way, nothing bad is ever gonna' happen, not in my life-time, anyway!"

All of us would like to believe that but there is just one problem with that. Governments and emergency responders all over the world are making preparations…for something.

News agencies have also been covering the topic of disaster preparedness a little too frequently for comfort. At some point or another, we might want to turn aside from our tabloid gossip, designer labels, and reality-shows, and pay attention. And then there is this little problem:

Revelations 8:8-9
Then the second angel sounded, and something like **a great mountain burning** with fire **was thrown into the sea,** and one third of the sea became blood...and **one third of the ships were destroyed.** And the name of the star is Wormwood.

Now, this is either the scribbling of some old man who drank too much 'vino 2,000 years ago...or an asteroid.

While you're thinking it over, let's review one possible scenario that might be of interest to all of us.

Discover Magazine reported as recently as June, 2007, that there are approximately 1,100 pesky **Near Earth Objects (NEO)** tumbling about aimlessly inside our galaxy, some measuring one kilometer in diameter. The article went on to state that each of these tumbling potatoes has the energy (a polite way of saying 'nuclear explosion power') equivalent to one million megatons of dynamite.

The consequence of just one NEO colliding with Earth would cause a series of calamities. First, an 'impact winter' would engulf the Earth and darken the sun, causing worldwide loss of life and crops, followed by starvation, disease, and chaos. The article also claimed that stronger impacts could cause the extinction of all known life forms on Earth.

Back in 2004, NASA and the world at large, believed none of the known asteroids in our galaxy presented any real threat to civilization but recently the agency issued this statement:

"We have no way of predicting future impacts."

Then in March of 2007, NASA published an equally alarming tidbit during its annual *Summary and Recommendations From ALAA Planetary Defense Conference,* held at George Washington University, D.C.

On Day 4 of the conference, astronomers reported they are "currently tracking 4,600 civilization killer NEO" loafing about our galaxy, and that they are "just beginning to find the dangerous ones."

The astronomers also warned that the impact could occur "with little or no warning" and would "exceed anything ever faced by recent civilization."

Suspiciously, this matches something Jesus of Nazareth described two thousand years earlier. Take a look:

Matthew 24:21
And then, there will be great tribulation, such as the world has never known, nor ever will know again.

What kind of an event can pull together the entire human race into one, unified terror? Why, everyone would have to lay down their guns and do a group hug.

And let's not forget about Little Apophis, Asteroid No. 99942. Measuring at just 278 meters across, it's the first known NEO that will fly by Earth, uncomfortably too close, in the year 2012, and again in 2029, but presents a real threat of impact on April 13, 2036. (The author's birthday. Gee thanks.)

All things considered, the description written by the aging Apostle John two thousand years ago becomes a little more interesting. Could an asteroid be the "burning mountain" spoken of in Revelations Chapter 8 that causes "one third" of global damage?

Any one of our oceans could provide this type of projectile the perfect triangulated coordinates that it needs to send tidal waves in all directions, and destroy one third of the Earth's ship yards dotted along the coasts. The impact would also poison "one third of all ocean life" due to radiation fallout.

The problem is, the Apostle said that as soon as the first one hits, a second one falls out of the sky, right after that. So, how much will the second one destroy? A few chapters later, he describes the destruction of the entire globe.

Whatever the case may be, NASA warns that these Near Earth Objects (NEO) can actually wipe us out.

Jet Propulsion Laboratories (JPL) of Pasadena, California, gives us an indication of how real the possibility of an undetected NEO can be. In 2007, the agency published an article on its *'Asteroids & Comets'* website, with this cheery pop quiz:

Did you know?…Asteroids are small, have very little gravity, and are hard to see in space because their rocky surfaces don't reflect a lot of light.

Well no, actually we didn't know all that, but thanks for the heads-up, JPL. Confirming the point, NASA adds:

"In almost all cases, we will either have a long lead-time or none at all."

Oddly, the NASA website where we obtained this information has been taken down, and replaced with this:

Forbidden
You don't have permission to access
/solar_system/asteroids_comets/ on this server.

It now appears that no matter what funding we devote or what telescopes we build to track these tumbling potatoes, civilization may never see it coming. Thankfully, the U.S. Congress considers this type of threat serious enough to read NASA's reports annually, and fund the agency's preemptive programs. Furthermore, just this past year, several scientists introduced new data suggesting December 21, 2012, as the new doomsday to watch for.

But seriously folks, whether an asteroid is coming or not, life goes on until then, and we need to invest in a good life insurance policy.

Christ Jesus gives them away for free, and there is never a premium or deductible to pay.

Something is about to happen and we all know it. We can feel that end-time clock ticking in our gut. The point is this: next time you hear some preacher shouting that God creates disasters to punish us, try to remember some of the cheeky backtalk in this book...

As though your life depends on it.

Psalms 91

Live under the protection of God Most High
And stay under His all-powerful shadow
Before long, you will say, "Yes, you really are my fortress,
And my place of safety; You are my God and I trust You."
The Lord will keep you safe from deadly traps and diseases.
He will spread His wings over you and keep you safe.
His faithfulness is like a shield, like a city wall.
You won't need to worry about terrors creep at night
Or weapons that fire during the day.
You will not be harmed!
Although thousands will fall all around you, you will only see it
With your eyes. The danger will not come near you.
The Lord Most High is your fortress, you can run to Him for
safety.
God will command his Angels to protect you wherever you go.
In fact, they will carry you in their arms, in case you so much
as stub your toe.
With God on your side, He will overpower anything that tries
to come up against you.
The Lord says, "If you acknowledge Me and truly get to know
Me, I will rescue you and keep you safe at every turn."
He also promises, "Whenever you are in trouble, you can call
out to Me, and I will answer you."
And then, He said the most astounding thing:
"I will protect you and honor you. You will live a long life and
see my saving power."

Thank you for joining us
in this frank and informative discussion.

To correspond with Selma Kerren
or purchase additional copies, write:

ocbeach949@gmail.com